Willful Virgin

Essays in Feminism
1976-1992

by
Marilyn Frye

The Crossing Press
Freedom, CA 95019

Library of Congress Cataloging-in-Publication Data

Frye, Marilyn.
    Willful virgin : essays in feminism, 1976-1992 / by
Marilyn Frye.
                p. cm.
    Includes bibliographical references.
    ISBN 0-89594-554-1 (cloth). — ISBN 0-89594-553-3 (paper)
    1. Feminist theory. 2. Feminism—United States. 3. Lesbian-
ism—United States. 4. Radicalism—United States. I. Title.
HQ1190.F79 1992
    305.42—dc20   92-16364
                                                        CIP

Acknowledgements

In the fifteen years spanned by these essays, I have been sustained and inspired by co-workers and interlocutors in a rich complex of overlapping and interconnected communities of thought and action. Carolyn Shafer has been my primary and loving relatum throughout, my main co-thinker. She has contributed substantial ideas and insights and has blessed me with her sturdy, reliable, and intelligent encouragement and criticism. She helps keep me grounded, and helps me fly. It is a good thing for feminism that Carolyn, whose vocation is not writing, talks frequently to a writer.

In the last several years, I have learned so much from María Lugones that I can't possibly keep track of it—about feminism, politics, friendship, and philosophy. I want to thank her for her persistence. I am grateful to Claudia Card and Sarah Lucia Hoagland for their writing, and for inspiration, criticism, and support, as well as long-haul friendship.

Certain other writers have also influenced my thinking in ways that cannot be acknowledged piecemeal in footnotes. I am indebted to the works of bell hooks, Andrea Dworkin, Mary Daly, and most recently, the Milan Women's Bookstore Collective. I am also more indebted than my footnotes indicate to the writing of Linda Alcoff, Gloria Anzaldúa, Marilyn Murphy, Catharine A. MacKinnon, Julia Penelope, and Naomi Scheman.

The Center for the Study of Women in Society at the University of Oregon and the Center for Advanced Feminist Studies at the University of Minnesota supported me through passages of this work, and I want especially to acknowledge women who created these centers and keep them alive. To name only a few of them with whom I have had the pleasure of working: Joan Acker, Shirley Nelson Garner, Ruth-Ellen Boetcher Joeres, Miriam Johnson, and Toni McNaron.

Finally, I must mention the Women's Studies students at Michigan State University, and the women in my lesbian community, who give me so much and are so appreciative of what I give them.

Lansing, Michigan
May 1992

Contents

Introduction

M y work, like that of many feminist writers/artists/philosophers, has been a persistent project of weaving a matrix of meanings, a world of sense, a symbolic order, in which I can place myself and in which I and all women have original (not relational or derivative), positive, liveable meaning. In the Patriarchal Universe of Discourse (PUD), women cannot have original, positive, liveable meaning, and according to the story the Patriarchal Universe of Discourse tells about itself, it is total: phallocratic culture is culture, the male symbolic is meaning, PUD is the world of sense. According to PUD, this feminist project, then, is inconceivable and impossible.[1]

In my first book, *The Politics of Reality*, I was exposing PUD's arrogant construction of itself as exhausting all sense, and I was locating the edges, gaps, and incoherencies of that world, in order to know in a useful and articulate way that PUD is not all the world there is or ever could be. I was claiming the possibility of other worlds, but not yet saying much about how we will make them, how we are making them. So most of the work in *Politics* is responsive in a general way to men's oppression of women, but is not to a great extent shaped as responses to particular issues or to other feminists' initiatives. In contrast, most of the writing in this new collection came into being as responses to other people's (all but one of them women's) projects or topics, or to events or problems in my various communities of identity and/or work. In reviews, responses, commentaries, and writings which address topics set by others, my own analysis and world-construction come through in a relatively diffuse and unsystematic way, but also in a way that reveals more of how my own life and invention respond to and are integrated and interwoven with others' lives and inventions. And in this interaction (as one might have predicted, since the creation of meaning is a social affair) the concrete project of construction, as opposed to the analytic project of "deconstruction," comes more to the fore.

The theme of separation is conspicuous in these essays and reviews, as it was in *Politics*. But now it is clearer to me that the separation that is most significant for women is the separation of women from women which is accomplished by the institutions and values of PUD—most obviously the institutions of female heterosexuality, racism, and economic stratification, but also, for example, liberal values that set male models of citizenship and participation in "the world" as the standard for women. Isolated from each other, and not being authors of meaning, women are all alike—that is, women are interchangeable blanks bearing meanings and distinctions which originate in PUD. Our original being and our differences arise simultaneously in our collective construction of a world of sense which recognizes women. The politics of the Willful Virgin is separatist, as opposed to assimilationist, but it is not focussed on separation; it is focussed on connection, on the relations among women which sustain radical invention—of ourselves, of sense, of worlds that are not PUD. And it supposes that without differences among women, there is no relation among women. Our differences are at the core of the possibility of making such worlds.[2]

To make a difference (to Make Difference, one might say), women have to do impossible things and think impossible thoughts, and that is only done in community. Without a community of sense, an individual cannot keep hold of her radical insights; she becomes confused, she forgets what she knew. Meanings only exist in systems of sense (in "symbolics," according to one current way of speaking). A thread of memory requires a fabric of thought to be lodged in. An individual's memory requires a collective memory to be lodged in. We call each other to creative acts of courage, imagination, and memory, but they are literally impossible without a community of women which recognizes and authorizes women's initiatives. Overtly or indirectly, all of these essays are about women in community.

As U.S. women of color and jewish women have been

saying to white women and christian-cultured women, and lesbians have been saying to nonlesbians, fat women to thin women, and on and on: one cannot create anything new without knowing oneself well as a participant in the political and semantic order one would undermine, abandon, displace, or dismantle. I am white, middle-class from birth, highly educated, christian-raised, a deviant woman. I am interested in knowing in detail how I enact these placements in PUD, how I practice my race and class, how my values and my way of being in the world align my energies with grand projects of domination, and what meanings all that gives to my transgressions. A theme of self-knowledge, of owning one's character and competence in PUD (wherever one is positioned in it), runs through these essays in counterpoint with the theme of creating new placements in new orders.

It is widely believed among intellectuals these days that PUD (and its material manifestation) is a construction of human social life, and not a "given" or a "natural order." This ontological commitment (which is, of course, no more *a priori* justifiable than the naturalism or essentialism it replaces) opens *everything* to political critique and to change. "Social constructionism" is supposed to be a doctrine of freedom which replaces a doctrine of determinism. Much of what I have been trying to do both in my life and in my writing, is to take the measure of that freedom. What freedom, exactly, and for whom, and by what labor can it be exercised? The willful virgin of the title essay is pushing the limits, and her community and impossible inventiveness serve for me, for now, as a sort of icon exemplifying the exercise of ontological freedom. The willful creation of new meaning, new loci of meaning, and new ways of being, together, in the world, seems to me in these mortally dangerous times the best hope we have.

[1] "PUD" is due to Julia Penelope.

[2] This and the subsequent paragraph reflect my reading of *Sexual Difference*, The Milan Women's Bookstore Collective (Bloomington, IN: Indiana University Press, 1990).

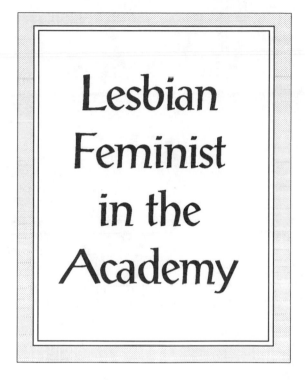

Lesbian Feminist in the Academy

Getting it Right[1]

1992

Once upon a time it was possible to use the terms 'politically correct' and 'politically incorrect' non-ironically, the former as a term of positive evaluation, the latter as a term of negative evaluation. This is not to say that those who used these terms non-ironically always used them simply to express an honest judgment: the terms also were used rhetorically as instruments of embrace and repudiation, inclusion and exclusion, to mark boundaries of affiliation, engage in dominance displays, and so on. And they were sometimes used ironically, with reversed valences. But in the recent national tempest about "diversity" and the canonical curriculum, the ironic reversal of values on these terms has been made so ubiquitous as to have actually changed their meanings, so that in common parlance 'politically correct' is a term of negative valuation signifying a praxis of righteous bullying combined with superficial and faddish political thought or program, a term generally employed as a deliberate insult; and 'politically incorrect' is a term of positive valuation generally used to express a snotty sort of pride in resistance or immunity to what is claimed to be the banal moralizing of the politically correct.[2] When people object to racism, sexism, etc., and recommend changes in behavior, they are accused of accusing others of being politically incorrect; but whether they are acting with integrity or not, they do not actually use the term 'politically incorrect' to characterize the things they object to—it is simply no longer available as a piece of non-ironic critical vocabulary.[3]

But perversely I persist in being able to hear the phrase

'politically correct' non-ironically and as a positive term. It sounds like a phrase I might have coined to name something I want to be—I want to "be political" and to get things right and not get them wrong. This seems to be the route both to my own narrow happiness and to my fullest possible positive engagement in the welfare and happiness of many others both near and distant. But to say I aspire to be politically correct must sound absurd or absurdly naive—or worse, merely cranky—unless some positive, non-ironic meaning can be pumped back into that term. I will not actually try to restore the term 'politically correct' to its (perhaps imaginary) former luster and usefulness, but I do want to ruminate about politics and "getting it right" in ways that at least suggest what the term 'politically correct' might mean if it were not just a curse. Then I will offer some views on the right (*versus* wrong, not *versus* left) politics of culture and curriculum.

Politics

It is useful for some purposes to think of the politics of a situation as like climate and weather, topology and soil: a multidimensional, multi-leveled, temporally extended, constantly changing, moving medium, a highly structured and fluid play of powers, which both sustains and threatens all the vital processes of human community existence; a sum of forces and pressures, currents, turbulences and calms, variations of density. The conditions of and in this medium at any particular time and place determine what can be done and by whom. That is, they determine and delimit the potential significance and effect of the actions and communications of agents who are variously located within and defined by it. Like the weather or climate, these conditions encourage or promote some social life processes and individual actions as they suppress or prohibit others, sometimes very generally over a wide spatio-temporal region, sometimes specifically or fleetingly. Conditions within this "socio-sphere" (conceived on analogy with the ecologist's "biosphere") also tend to generate, promote, suppress, or disperse other conditions within it. All states and processes in it and of it are interdependent.

No metaphor perfectly renders its field. This elemental metaphor suggests that the structures and flows of power are, like the weather, something that humans do not create and cannot control or alter beyond the fabrication of barriers and shelters. But the jet streams, thunderstorms, and sunshine of the socio-sphere are in fact products of human action, interaction and interpretation, and can be altered by human action, interaction, and interpretation.[4] Nevertheless, it is a benefit of this metaphor that it may attune the poet/philosopher/theorist to the fact that the whole unfathomably complex and fluid product of species-historic social construction, the planetary human life in which all human individuals are immersed, is not a "construct" like an artifact—like an automobile, for example—which can be tinkered with, dismantled, or demolished by an individual or a small work crew. It is not even like a very big artifact like the Sears Tower which can be demolished or structurally revised by concerted socially-organized marshalling of resources and labor. It is also not "beyond us" like a massive computer no one person understands, but whose plug we might pull. Considered in relation to our individual and collective grasps and our semantic and material technologies, the systems and plays of power that constitute us as collectives are much more like the weather than like these other socially created constructions. Projects of changing them have to be more like organic gardening than like factory retooling.

Given this metaphoric image of what politics is, I understand a person's politics to be in significant part a matter of alignment and affiliation. Likewise, the politics of any policy, practice, project, or way of doing things, or the politics of a group, organization, or institution, is in large part a matter of how it works to align and affiliate people. Acts and habits, policies and practices, ways of doing things—those of individuals and of all kinds of collectivities—direct and regulate the flow of people's energies and the other resources the people command. They join our energies to some of the currents of power in our situations, adding to the effect of both; they set our energies against some currents, generating friction which may strengthen or deplete either or both. Each person is aligned with and against and at various angles to various forces and currents, and in this each is with others—and not with other others. By virtue of one's own acts and one's places in collectives and their processes, one is a fellow-traveller with some and "part of the problem" to others; to some, one is both. Every aspect of one's life, no matter how trivial or local to oneself, is in some way (in many ways, simultaneously and not necessarily consistently) located in the currents and landscapes of politics and tends to reinforce or to alter some aspects of one's alignment and affiliation within that fluid structure. (Obvious examples of the sorts of alignments and oppositions in question are such things as where one shops—national chains or locally owned businesses, minority-owned businesses, etc.—and how and where one disposes of one's trash. Perhaps less obvious are such things as whom one greets and does not greet on the street, whether one is or is not engaged in grading and certifying students, to whom and at what provocation one donates money, how one uses humor in intra-group bonding rituals. But giving examples, here, can be misleading, since I am claiming that in fact everything one does and thinks, every attitude one strikes, everything one says, aligns one's energies and resources with and against various currents of power at various levels of social organization.)

People's politics—those of individuals and of groups—also have to do with their practical understanding of politics at all its levels and in all its complexity. The point and purpose of political understanding (I do not refer only to explicit or theoretical understanding but also to common sense, street smarts, taste, and other modes of being savvy) is to generate maps and instruments and good intuitions which guide individuals' and groups' negotiation and navigation in the currents of the sociosphere so that the net effect is to engage wills and resources in movement that enhances and furthers the well-beings of individuals, of groups, and of social-historic processes that it is good to enhance and further. The politics of anything is about will and value: aligning, allying, and engaging individual and collective will with that which is of value, which includes engaging will in the making of value.[5] Political understanding should contribute to getting this connection of will and value right.[6] (If a person or group or process is getting it right in part by virtue of a sound working understanding of the politics of a situation, we could say—but we can't, of course—that she/he/it is politically correct.)

But political understanding and the right alignments and affiliations are difficult to achieve.

I suppose that virtually everyone lives constantly, almost from birth, with some understanding, more or less adequate or accurate, of the local politics of their situations. As Bob Dylan observed, it doesn't take a weatherman to know which way the wind blows.[7] We are attuned to what powers we command and what powers will be directed by others for us and against us, and we negotiate the currents both intuitively and deliberately like a white-water canoeist or a sailor in high and shifting winds. A great deal of this multi-layered and context-sensitive knowledge seems to be with us like the perceptions we have of our physical environments by way of peripheral vision. In both cases, a constant flow of invaluable and highly interpreted information is readily available to us and we rely on it spontaneously and faithfully, while very rarely taking explicit cognizance of it. People everywhere know "by the seat of their pants" a great deal of the intricacy of local politics. We operate intelligently and quite effectively with and within that system of powers even when its main tendency is to disempower and disable us, even to disable us as perceivers and interpreters of our circumstances. But the many layers and structures on larger scales are not as readily perceived, interpreted, negotiated. Relative to the locus of a single awareness keyed to the specificities of a single life, such politics generally are diffuse, obscure, and remote. For one thing, they operate in ways that are causally complex and diffuse and they constitute blocks and channels that are not encountered experientially either as barriers or as externally engineered. (I refer, for example, to the many and intricately related remote causes of the needs and fears at play in the politics of the average academic department office, and to the many forces that construct appetites a person experiences as elementally and personally one's own or as just natural to human beings, e.g., who one finds congenial, whose love or alliance one needs, one's material desires and needs. Also, I am thinking of such things as barriers to social intercourse across ages, races, ethnic communities, religions, and so on, which often influence people very decisively without ever being recognized as barriers.) In addition, the regional, continental, and global prevailing winds, currents, fronts, storms, and seasons of power—macroscopic phenomena—are obscure because they are obscured: they are veiled and disguised by those in the most powerful groups through the services of their willing or unwitting propagandists (among whom should be counted most professors, members of the clergy, professionals, and participants in the production of mass media). Active promotion of various kinds of error and false consciousness about political structures, processes, and forces is integral to some of the operations of power.[8] And what makes the task of political understanding even more difficult is that we (at least U.S. persons within my own ken) are accustomed to locating larger scale causes by observing uniformities of effect: where something particular and local happens repeatedly in the same way, we postulate a common, more general cause. But in the case of politics (as, indeed, in the case of material weather) the currents of power do not have the same consequences for all the individuals and groups they affect, not even for all those similarly situated with respect to various institutions and categories. To intuit the politics of a situation one has to sense and think quite differently than one does in diagnosing, for instance, the causes of the repeated occurrence of a certain ailment in a certain population of schoolchildren.[9]

For these and other reasons, patient and skillful observation and acute intuition are required to recognize and understand the politics of a situation, even though some aspects of it, especially aspects that operate at a local, microscopic level, are quite obvious and familiar. It is often not at all obvious which acts and policies of individuals or collectives will in fact align and ally them as they would—or should—want to be aligned and allied.

In the Academy

Suppose you are a person seriously interested in minimizing your contribution to situations in which sentient beings suffer, and maximizing your contribution to the existence of sustainable situations of living that systematically promote their individual and collective thriving.[10] Or, suppose you are more modest or more parochial in your aspirations, and you commit yourself only to sustainable good circumstances for a group or category of folk with whom you identify; imagine that it is a group that has for some long time been subject to oppression, exploitation, ethnic or racial hatred, destruction of culture, or similar evils. Suppose you are a particular person situated in some particular time, place, and station. With what people, what trends and forces, what currents, what institutions should you align and ally yourself, and how could you accomplish such alignment and alliance?

I am someone with such aspirations, with both global

and parochial reference, and I am situated just so. Almost everyone on my campus who knows me or knows of me would categorize me as some sort of radical who could be counted upon to be on the "politically correct" side of every issue and, for example, to be in favor of affirmative action, curriculum integration,[11] and multiculturalism, and to align and ally myself with others who favor these things. Some think my support of and identification with such causes is dependable only because it is automatic, unreflective, "knee-jerk." But I cannot be counted on. In fact I am, very reflectively indeed, very uncertain about the projects and policies being pursued under these rubrics. Though I am well aware of some good outcomes for some people, such projects and policies are also risky and harmful in ways which their supporters (among which I can at least some of the time be counted) have not adequately assessed, and I suspect that the long-term political drift of these projects and policies may be regressive rather than progressive.

Let me rehearse some of these difficulties, which I am by no means the first to note.

Consider affirmative action in higher education student admissions and faculty hiring. Affirmative action hiring practices certainly have interrupted or prevented some cases of unjust or unfair closure to or elimination of job candidates. But affirmative action is most successful as a quite selective strategy of assimilation, co-optation and tokenism. It tends to induct into the "mainstream" the most assimilable individuals, those whose already-acquired skills, manners, accents, and values are most like or complementary to those of the people who are already securely ensconced in the academy.[12] Those who are not thus socialized become the multiple proofs that "qualified women and minorities" cannot be found. Hence, predictably, affirmative action has worked better to assimilate white middle- and upper-middle-class women into white-male-dominated education domains and professions than it has to assimilate African American, Asian, Latino, or Native American people; in many academic settings, the numbers of members of ethnic or racialized minorities have actually been decreasing in the last few years.

Furthermore, in the United States, beginning with the era of the Civil Rights Movement, educated and politicized women and men who are African American, Latino/a, or Native American, and educated and politicized white women of all classes, have constituted relatively active and resourceful populations of malcontents well-situated to assume leadership in movements for radical, transforming change that would drastically alter the distribution and flow of power. The opportunity for more education and an academic or professional career may draw members of these groups (and has drawn many) into activities, intellectual milieux, and lives which alienate them from those with whom they might have worked revolutionary change. This has worked especially well, in my opinion, for (or, more accurately, against) middle- and upper-middle class white women, as well as educationally advantaged white working-class women.

And the most stunning success of affirmative action has been as a strategy of tokenism: nearly every academic setting and activity includes one "woman" and/or one "minority," often enough in the body of one and the same person, which signals deceptively to all and sundry that if you behave well and "achieve," you can succeed, no matter what your race, sex, or national origin, and that the institution is indeed an "equal opportunity employer."

For those who cherish the status quo, such workings of affirmative action should be counted as goods. But in many cases they do not perceive this and they resist affirmative action. Their narrow perspectives and bigotry, and for some the self-serving belief that the traditional initiation processes have all along been democratic and merit-based, make them think of affirmative action as upsetting, rather than protectively adapting, the status quo. Because of this resistance, affirmative action policies and processes have to operate to a great extent by bureaucratic coercion, generating multi-step procedures, wasteful and irritating paper trails of documentation, and administrative policing (some of which is, itself, cynically permissive). They thus encourage and promote a climate of cynical manipulation of rules and of people, and they promote resentment and suspicion of those supposed to have benefited from the process.[13]

Affirmative action institutionally affirms and thus ever-more-deeply entrenches a liberal bureaucratic politics according to which (1) assimilating (some of) those who are marginalized into the "mainstream" is the way to resolve social problems of race, class and gender, (2) formal justice (e.g., publicly advertised job openings constituting formal equality of access to the job market) is all the justice that is needed, and (3) formal justice can be achieved by coercive and bureaucratic regulation of social processes. This is not a politics with which I willingly align myself. Currents in the socio-sphere that promote co-optation of potential change agents, tokenism, cynicism, and manipulation are not currents to which I happily join my energies.

Curriculum integration is the curricular version of affirmative action. The by-now-familiar idea is that the standard college and university curriculum covers a very narrow range of the cultural product of humans on this planet while presenting that slim product as identical with culture itself, and that it is desirable to introduce into that curriculum content that refers to a much wider range of cultural product and culture producers, that is, material by and about "women and minorities" and other marginalized or erased folk. It is thought, or hoped, that the integration (not mere addition) of that material will not leave the previous content intact, but will transform it.

Some people have critically noticed that in the process of curriculum integration scholars have quickly canonized (tokenized) a few cultural products and their producers through making them the standard representatives of the "other" that is to be integrated. Two other things seem less often attended to: the matter of how this process of integration will transform the "new" material; and the matter of the continued production of "new" material in cultural loci outside the arena of this transforming marriage of the traditional canon and the "other" knowledge. I fear a replication of Euro-American colonialism. European colonial cultures were profoundly affected and altered by their integration of the cultures of the peoples they conquered, but this "transformation," one of whose rather interesting products is contemporary U. S. culture, was not markedly beneficial to the cultural groups whose culture was being integrated. Integration of their cultural product into the "curriculum" of the colonizing culture was not a mechanism of emancipation for them. In fact, many such groups did not survive to the day when their members might benefit from seeing themselves reflected in the media and the arts of the transformed dominant culture (nor would those hapless individuals have recognized their reflection). I am concerned that women's studies, African-American studies and other ethnic or area studies—academic cultures that are providing the dominant academic culture with its "new" subjects, materials, and methods—might likewise not survive the transformation of the traditional curriculum.[14]

"Multiculturalism" has a sweeter sound to me than "affirmative action" or "curriculum integration."[15] It seems to affirm plurality instead of unification/co-optation by integration or assimilation. Most of the students and faculty members in U.S. universities in the present era need to be vastly more informed and appreciative of multiplicity, plurality, and diversity, both among and within cultures. Most of us lack and need deep and subtle understandings of the complexities of interaction and influence among cultures. Many of us need some profound encounters with some particular cultures beyond our own. These understandings and encounters seem to be the likely antidotes to racism, ethno-solipsism, and other destructive rigidities of thought and practice that lock us into alignment with currents of oppression, exploitation, imperialism, and many forms of habitual cruelty and abusiveness among ourselves. It seems to me highly desirable for students, faculty, and administrators to find and to create ways to turn the resources of colleges and universities to the encouragement of such learning. One significant historical/structural barrier to this is that most of the people in whose hands these resources and this project would be (or is) have themselves been socialized as cultural thieves and exoticists. They may not be able to figure out (and will not be able to seek and accept suitable help in figuring out) how to promote appreciation of cultural plurality without promoting just more annihilative assimilation. These people, one should bear in mind, benefit continuously and in multiple ways from privileges they have and maintain at the expense of others, including precisely those others whose culture and work they might want to "integrate" or even to be transformed by. These people [we, they, you], one should not forget, grew up on *The National Geographic* and read The Nature Company and Banana Republic catalogues in the bathroom and in bed; they [we, you] are the direct descendants of the folks who conceived and created the African Hall in the American Museum of Natural History in New York City that communicates "abundantly about 20th century United States" but is "reticent, even mute, about Africa."[16]

To promote multiculturalism, and not cultural colonialism, requires that we promote a world in which there are multiple, thriving, relatively autonomous, mutually respectful and appreciative cultures (or other kinds of loci of social living and culture-making for which the term 'culture' might not be quite apt). In the microcosm of the U.S. academy, this translates into the necessity of cultivating and nurturing multiple nuclei of study, research, and creative activity that are not primarily "integrative" but rather are constructive projects of generating knowledge and generating culture at and beyond the boundaries of traditional and dominant disciplines, methods, and subject matters. Instead of allocating yet more resources to traditional disciplines presumably to reform them, resources should be channeled to programs of African-American studies, many programs of ethnic and area studies, women's studies, lesbian studies and gay studies, and special-focus programs in the disciplines and the arts, where the resources will support people and work that create, express, and articulate knowledges rooted in many different kinds of lives and circumstances.

The notion of multiculturalism is suggestive of novelty and change both for multiple programs and projects other than traditional disciplines and studies, and for those traditional activities as well. The creative powers of non-traditional projects will be released when they are recognized as having integrity of their own and are free not to refer constantly to main streams of Anglo-European culture, disciplinary canons, and standards of value that are already deeply engraved in the traditional curriculum, not even for the purpose of reforming or transforming them. And on the other hand, if people doing the research and scholarship that has been traditional in U.S. universities for a century or so were to recognize their subject matter as the products of quite specific cultures and situations—were to embrace their enterprise as one "area study" among others—they might well begin to understand and amplify the complex oppressive and liberatory, conservative and transgressive, currents in the materials and circumstances they already study, the culture they already participate in constructing. The traditional curriculum might be rediscovered, or re-construed, in ways that preserve it from being an exercise in cultural chauvinism and/or cultural imperialism, and the culture it expresses and helps to construct might be both invigorated and made nontoxic to other cultures. Participants in these enterprises then could with integrity claim the same respect that is being claimed by the people and works they formerly erased, marginalized, and/or colonized. Those who perceive that their own power is preserved by the traditional way of doing the traditional curriculum will want to resist such a reconception of their work, of course.

The notion of multiculturalism also suggests a changed understanding of the campus. It cannot continue to be conceived as a relatively closed and self-contained place where scholars, researchers, and artists are cloistered. There still are many habits and policies in universities that serve to restrict the mobility of members of university communities, to restrict primary physical locales of our work to college campuses, requiring us to be "in residence" a great deal of the time and imposing barriers to our taking "leaves." An interest in multiculturalism would suggest allocating more resources to travel, and enacting generous practices regarding leaves-of-absence for scholars (both faculty and students) whose projects require physical removal from campuses and physical presence in other sites of human living. (I am thinking not so much of scholars visiting "other's" cultures, as of scholars working in the various locales of their own cultures.) It would also suggest much more various and generous definitions of "research" and "scholarship."

To sum up, the notion of multiculturalism seems to me to imply a very different picture of the university or college than that implied by the notion of curriculum integration (or even transformation). Integration suggests a flow to already-existing centers and an evolution of a single all-purpose complex that "reflects" everyone approximately equally and meets the educational needs of all different sorts of people. Multiculturalism suggests a flow that is governed by a plurality of centers of gravity, and the evolution of a system with no center. And it suggests a picture of universities as things not run hierarchically by business-management principles. These are things most administrators and faculty members—even the "tenured radicals"—neither envisage nor want.

Getting it Right

The reflections that make me ambivalent about support of the apparently progressive initiatives in academia do lead me to revise my relatively jolly suggestion that "correct" is what I want my politics—those alignments and alliances—to be.

"Correcting" a situation seems to be precisely what is

attempted by means such as affirmative action and curriculum integration projects. To correct is to bring something into conformance with pre-established rule; it pertains to regimentation; it has to do with the perception of something as deviant or deviating from some rule or norm and manipulations of some sort to bring it into line. The power struggle in the academy has to do with who is going to determine what the "rule" is; practices within the institutions will proceed by the same logic of correction, whoever gets to set the rule. Thinking of a sound, loving, pluralistic politics as "correct" may not help one divorce oneself from thinking by such a logic.

For those of us who would like to contribute to the end of the world regime of oppression, I think it is counterproductive to try directly to control (correct) the actions and processes (such as practices and curricula in the academy) that contribute to constituting and maintaining the present climate. The metaphor of politics as weather and climate suggests that coercion, regulation, seduction, even persuasion (which it is difficult to distinguish from coercion)[17] are too narrow, too mechanical, and too specifically adapted to the inner workings of a specific local system to be ways of directing energies and wills to profound and structural change. The politics of knowledge and culture I favor is a practice that minimizes adversarial, coercive, and/or reformist engagement (struggle) with established institutions and disciplines, and frees one's energy for maintaining, strengthening, and creating other knowledges. The politics of the university I favor is one which frees students, scholars, researchers and artists for such preservation and creativity.

A person situated roughly as I am (like many if not most other academics in the United States), with aspirations such as I have owned here, is not well-advised to try to reform the "traditional curriculum" of universities or of Western culture. She is better advised to join others in committing herself to practices of new construction. As for the question of whether I am getting it right when I promote such a politics of separation, creation, and autonomy, I cannot, of course, be certain. But I am quite sure such a politics at least does not get it wrong in the same old way.

[1] This was written as a contribution to a Forum on "political correctness" in SIGNS: Journal of Women in Culture and Society, the Summer issue of 1992. I am grateful to the editors of SIGNS, Ruth-Ellen Boetcher Joeres and

Barbara Laslett, for giving me such an occasion to collect my thoughts on this matter, and such an opportunity to air them.

[2] This reversal of meanings is reminiscent of Nietzsche's analysis of morality and his eagerness to be "immoral" or amoral—to be free of a morality that is designed and promoted specifically to weaken the oppressed. At least since Nietzsche's time, any moral argument for change and any political strategy of taking the moral high ground is liable to this kind of backlash, either earnestly or cynically deployed.

[3] The disappearance of items of critical vocabulary should not go unremarked, for it tends to suppress criticism. It interests me that some of the folks who happily ironize *this* vocabulary to flatness are themselves most upset with postmodernists who, they suppose, would ironize the meaning out of their own favorite critical vocabulary (*truth, knowledge, individual, objective, real, man, necessary*, etc.).

[4] I do not mean they are pure products of human construction. I am not a neo-idealist sort of constructionist. For instance, I think that although nowadays famines are socially constructed, the fact that plants capable of providing human nutrition generally do not grow abundantly in deserts is not. The construction and politics of famine would be different if they did.

[5] Sarah Hoagland's *Lesbian Ethics* (Palo Alto, Calif: Institute of Lesbian Studies, 1988) presents lesbian community as a partly deliberate project of creating value, as opposed to just aligning ourselves with or against values in a preexisting scheme of value.

[6] When I speak of what it is good to enhance and further, I recognize that there is not agreement about what *is* good to enhance and further. An individual (I, for example) may think she has some grasp of what is good; and she will approve of politics which connect wills to the promotion of those good things. People might agree with me in this account of what politics is, but identify incompatibly different politics as "getting it right."

[7] To give some examples from my own culture and time: A black male suspected of shoplifting in a suburban mall has little chance of avoiding being perceived and treated as an incorrigible criminal; a white male, even one whose age and class status put him somewhat at risk, has a better chance. And virtually all Black males and all white males know this from a very young age, whether or not they have thought it through at an articulate level. Children know who they can get in trouble by saying certain things about them to certain people. Women know how to get what they want by convincing men it is what the men want (a strategy which has its limits, as the history of reformist feminism shows). I take such things to be examples of people's knowledge of the politics of their situations.

[8] At the local level people also take advantage of opportunities to manipulate others' perceptions of what is going on and they often enough succeed magnificently, but at that level and scale it is easier to detect and correct for deceit.

[9] For another discussion of this point, see Marilyn Frye, *The Politics of Reality: Essays in Feminist Theory* (Freedom, Calif: The Crossing Press, 1983) "Introduction," xi-xiii.

[10] There is no difficulty in your affirming that thriving may consist of different things for different people, and you need not assume you can know just what will conduce to whose welfare. You need not be arrogant or patronizing.

[11] *Curriculum integration,* in my neck of the woods, refers to syllabus-revision projects aimed at incorporating materials by and about people other than elite racially privileged males in courses. It has been used most, in my hearing, in reference more specifically to including (integrating, not merely adding) materials by and about women in the syllabi of courses which hitherto contained only material by men and generated from men's perspectives.

[12] For instance, my own life and career have been directly and decisively affected by institutional affirmative action; without it, I almost surely would not have been in the academy for so many years. But I am so highly assimilable that it is shocking that a corrective such as affirmative action was even necessary. Though I am a woman (which is the misfortune that affirmative action was needed to neutralize) and a lesbian, I am Anglo-Saxon, Christian-cultured, born-and-bred middle class, silver-spoon educated, and generally pass as "normal" in appearance and manner, at least in academic settings.

[13] I do not think you can make significant changes without occasioning some resentment and suspicion, not to say hostility, but I do think one should anticipate this cost and attempt to ensure that one is getting something for it.

[14] It does not comfort me that substantial private and government funding is available for curriculum integration projects.

[15] But I am sobered by the news that in the university I work at the term "affirmative action" has become *lingua non grata* among those who are institutionally responsible for promoting "diversity," and that the term "multiculturalism" is now preferred. If it is just a new name for the old policies, this linguistic shift is not good. Only time will tell whether this marks, rather, a real shift in those people's vision and understanding of what they want to be promoting.

[16] Donna J. Haraway, *Primate Visions: Gender, Race and Nature in the World of Modern Science* (NY: Routledge, 1989), 27.

[17] Cf., Joyce Trebilcot, "Dyke Methods," *Lesbian Philosophies and Cultures,* edited by Jeffner Allen (Albany, New York: State University of New York Press, 1990), 15-29.

Who Wants
A Piece of The Pie?[1]
1976

For feminists, the permanent moral problem of how to live becomes the problem of how to live in accord with feminist values; we have to subsist by means which are harmonious with these values, and we have to live well enough to have resources for change and for enduring processes and events precipitated by our own movement. In short, we need more than subsistence, we are committed to getting it in wholesome ways, and we must manage all of this now, within a hostile sexist society. Looking about at people's lives generally, it seems that requiring more than subsistence is a considerable luxury, and so it can seem that a feminist ethic which presupposes that luxury is necessarily elitist. There is truth in this, but it is not the last word. For one thing, revolution may in fact *be* something of a luxury—its moment is not to be found among the absolutely destitute. And furthermore, if having resources beyond the requirements of material subsistence is deemed a luxury, then a great many of us were born to that luxury as surely as we were born to our oppression as women, and we had better understand what it means and what we should do with it.

For some of us these dilemmas rise concretely in the matters of work and privilege. One apparently rich resource which many feminists have, have access to, or aspire to, is a situation in an establishment institution or profession. Attractions include salaries, fringe benefits, offices and supplies, postage, secretarial services and assistants, transportation services, contacts with other persons similarly situated, and respectability. But there are feminists who have been wary of this, and have been inclined to reject such situations or aspirations, as part of their rejection of class privilege.

Elimination of class privilege, along with race privilege, is certainly a feminist goal; if we ignore it we will find ourselves outmaneuvered by a strategy of sex-integration in middle bureaucracy, which would strengthen white middle-class dominance and divert the force of radical feminism. Part of our defense against this is steady awareness of class and race. Class privilege is offensive; but *privilege* is itself an odd sort of self-regenerative thing which, once you've got it, cannot be simply shucked off like a too-warm jacket.

Privilege in general is maintained by its exercise. It must remain substantially unquestioned by the non-privileged and this is achieved through the constant, easy, more-or-less unconscious exercise of it. The constancy and the ease make it seem *natural*, and then render it almost imperceptible, like the weight of one's clothes on one's body. As a consequence of this, one cannot *merely* do something which *happens* to be a privilege to be able to do. The "mere" exercise of the privilege positively contributes to the continuance of privilege. Using it strengthens it. This obviously applies to taking a position in an establishment institution: taking such a job not only uses privilege but builds privilege. And even this is not the worst of it. For, to reject the position is also to exercise privilege. As a matter of fact, it seems more of a privilege to be able to *turn down* a $15,000-a-year administrative job than to be in a position to get it in the first place. If the question even arises for a particular woman, then she *has* privilege; and she cannot refrain from having it, whichever decision she then makes. In deciding not to do some lucrative thing one is privileged to do, one is falling back on *other* privileges. The person who does not take the $15,000 job can handle the resulting poverty relatively well because the same skills, training, connections and style which fit her for the job, enable her to be a reasonably crafty consumer and manipulator of bureaucratic process, and give her a network of well-connected acquaintances; and she starts out her poverty in good health and forearmed with feminist analysis. For most people, poverty is intolerably destructive; for most people, choosing it would be choosing a form of suicide. Having relative poverty as a genuine and interesting option is itself a privilege.

I see no way to suddenly stop having privilege, or to

stop exercising it. I certainly am not saying that privilege is ineradicable absolutely—but one cannot suddenly, by a simple act of will, detach oneself from it (which is perhaps one of the many reasons why "personal" solutions are inadequate). And in the end, if poverty and detachment from establishment institutions would eventually reduce one to having no privilege it is still far from obvious that feminists should do it. To renounce middle-class privilege is not to extricate oneself from the system but to relocate oneself within it. Joining the lower classes and recruiting members to them may tend more to the support of the system than to its downfall, for it may simply be providing more victims for the more thorough exploitation and oppression which take place at the lower levels of the hierarchy: those more thoroughly oppressed provide more fuel for the machinery.[2]

Impoverishment and deprivation *reduce* power, vision and endurance. The idea that Justice and Dignity require Suffering belongs to an ethic of self-denial, a slave morality. All resource is tainted (men have not yet been dispossessed). We recognize this and we aim to change it. Meanwhile it is not politically incorrect to avail ourselves of the resources available to us.

If the foregoing arguments are sound, then holding a well-paying job is not necessarily in violation of feminist principles. Since virtually all well-paying jobs are establishment jobs, the next rack of problems is generated by *tokenism*. In virtually all middle-income, middle-bureaucracy, middle-civil-service jobs, a woman will be a token woman, since virtually none of these are classified as "women's work." Her existence there as a token woman works for the good of the institution and the ill of women generally. The presence of the token is used to convince both her employers and the rest of the world that the institution is not sexist and need not bother seriously with affirmative action, or correcting salary inequities or sexist division of work, et cetera, while it cheerfully continues to hire and promote men and serve male interests. These goods done the institutions are complemented by various harms done the token woman (one never gets something for nothing). The token woman is generally quite isolated; she will not have the relations with her colleagues that the men have, and thus the whole work situation is not as rich in stimulation, assistance, and comradeship as it is for most men in similar positions. This is likely to affect the quality of her work, or the amount of energy it takes to maintain the quality of her work. And this isolation also aggravates the constant problem of coping with the difficult questions of integrity and compromise that arise for her. She has to decide whether and in what degree she must be a closet feminist, how manly to act in order to be taken seriously, how much, when, where and with whom to fight over sexist language, sexist jokes, sexist gallantry, sexist assumptions, sexism in hiring and promotion and such consummate evils as sexist dress requirements. If a woman fails to take matters of integrity and compromise seriously, or makes the wrong decisions, she is likely to slip into being one of the boys—a female man. If she takes them seriously and makes the right decisions, she invites the fate of being a *token feminist*, and the whole situation becomes more complicated. My situation as a professor at a university exemplifies this nicely.

Sometimes I catch a glimpse of myself in a classroom, in a university building, clothed and fed and insured by the university, before an audience brought there by the university; and I am very seriously spelling out and explaining for them as persuasively as I can a radical feminist perception of the world, and coaching them in the arts of right reason and clear vision so they will be able to discover for themselves what is going on in this sexist culture. And the better I am at teaching these things, the more truth I find and communicate, the more good I do the institution. The fact that it allows someone to stand in it and say those things gives it credit in the eyes of the students and the wider public. That I am there saying truths and teaching women makes the whole thing more tolerable for the women. The better I am, the better they feel about being in the university, the more they are inclined to believe that professors know what they are talking about, the more they feel the university really is a place where knowledge will bring them freedom. And the stronger is the institution. But among the truths is the truth that the institution is male-dominated and directed to serve the ends of a male-dominated society, economy and culture. As such, its existence, not to mention its strength and vigor, is inimical to the welfare of women, and probably to the survival of the species. If the women in the class come to agree with me in belief and perception, they must see me then as an absurd figure. For I am just that. I can try to see myself as someone working as an undercover agent, fomenting restlessness and stirring up radical sentiment and anger, working as a traitor from within, as an agent of the new order.... But that gratifying fantasy is absurdly counterbalanced by the fact that I am doing all this fomenting quite openly, *in the pay* of the institution, with the blessing of the patriarchy, in the context of a grading system, and with the students learning through all of this that the university is a good place, a place where freedom reigns. The university is in the business of authority; by bestowing its authority on selected token representatives of non-standard views, it enhances its own authority, which is used and designed to be used in the maintenance and justification of male hegemony over knowledge.[3]

Tokenism is painful, and either resolution of the problems of integrity and compromise—joining the boys or becoming a token feminist—immerses the woman in the absurdity. For the token feminist, the thing must eventually come down to the question of when, over what issues, and with what provocation to fight the battle which will lose her job; or when to reject the absurdity and resign. It is inevitable that it comes to this question. If she is a feminist her tolerance for sexist abuse must have a limit; if she is unable or unwilling to risk her job, she has no limit; if she can risk it she eventually will.

The conclusion here is, of course, that a feminist should not be too dependent upon her establishment job. And this is not peculiar to establishment jobs; anyone living and acting in a manner calculated to bring about changes in her situation must keep her options open. Economic flexibility is needed by anyone who is sticking to some principles. But there are factors contributing to dependence which are of particular significance to a feminist working an establishment job—especially in the kind of emotive or psychological relationship one has to the institution in which one works.

I began to see these questions of relationship through discussion with another woman professor about the role and life of a feminist in such a position. There was much agreement, until we got to the question of reforming the university. She claimed the university's ideals were fine and it could be made to live up to them; that one should work for reform in the institution, and this would help reform society. I claimed that these "ideals" were not really the university's ideals at all but a public relations hype, and it was never meant to live up to them and never would. What emerged was a crucial and profound difference of *affect*, not of opinion. She was *loyal* to the university and its professed ideology, she had *faith* in the institution; I had neither faith nor loyalty. As she talked, it became clear that her loyalty was rather like filial love or patriotism. I have seen such loyalty also among those who have worked for a long time for one of the large paternalistic corporations.

The pathology of institutional loyalty seems to come from at least three sources. First, the institution keeps the person on the payroll, increasing salary and benefits a little faster than the cost of living goes up. Second, there is the matter of exclusivity, of fraternal bonding, especially in loyalty to a profession. This has a nice additional twist when the subject, a sister, is being taken in as a brother. A third source of loyalty lies in the fact that one gains status and identity from one's position in an established institution, profession, or the like. One *is* a professor; one *is* a physician; one *is* the director of the women's studies program. The bestower of such meaning and identity is the bestower of self-respect, of personhood (or so it seems to the love-struck employee). One is grateful, and indebted, almost as to one's heavenly creator.

An institution, profession, corporation or such, to which one feels loyal, which one loves, has a great deal more than mere economic power over one. The threat of being fired, in one form or another, is laced with overtones of the threat of rejection by a loved one, ostracism by the brotherhood, and annihilation through loss of identity. I believe that for mere mortals these are irresistible forces.

The various sorts of dependence upon institutions which can undermine the feminist's ability to make proper use of an establishment employment as a resource for herself and the movement bear a rather obvious similarity to the sorts of dependence the stereotypic wife has on the stereotypic husband. She is tied to him by economic necessity and by feelings of owing him loyalty because he supports her, and she loves him because she derives her sense of meaning, her identity and status from his gracious association with her. The first salvation of woman from her fallen state, through her love and marriage to prince Charming, was a disaster; re-marrying prince Charming now, deceptively clothed as a title and a good salary, would be a disaster of the same magnitude and type.

It is, I find, a fundamental difference between me and

many other feminists I know as colleagues, that I judge the opposition of interests between women and sexist (misogynist) institutions to be such that we can be united with them in matrimony or brotherhood, or alienated from them in sisterhood. The duality is so sharp because these anti-woman institutions offer (or pretend to offer) livelihood and identity, and women, the dispossessed and invisible, are dying for these. As a consequence of this the integrity of a feminist working within such an institution must depend on her alienation from it and the constancy of her adversarial relation with it. This orientation is maintained, not negatively through resistance of temptation or a system of coercive pressures and checks from other feminists, but positively, through woman-loving.

This woman-loving that supports one's spiritual independence of the establishment institutions, supports best if it is not closeted. The publicity of a primary and loving identification with women places one in a position both with respect to the agents of the institution and with respect to other women, of having to live up to it or be a fool or a fake. And the openness of one's woman-loving feminism is necessary also to be realizing one of the most important benefits one's own establishment employment can have for other women. This is the benefit of space in which they can be women and feminists without fatal opposition and deprecation. One's status, authority, recognition and power, however modest, are conveyed to those with whom one is identified. Respectability, like guilt, travels by association, without specific effort and without specific control; and respectability purchases space. Every time one woman moves or acts, she makes room for other women to move, to act, to be—*if* her womanness is overtly present as a salient factor in the situation, and *not if* she is masquerading as a man or a neuter.

The material benefits of establishment jobs include the income, the insurance, the access to duplicating machines and space for meetings, the material support of one's feminist work through use of paid "company-time" for work, organizing, proselytizing, etc. One can and should share the wealth and resource within the community of feminists through income-sharing, use and support of membership in feminist operations such as credit unions, health clinics, woman's centers, bookstores and so on. And one's position and whatever accumulation of savings it makes possible can serve a community, and not just

one person or one household, as a sort of cushion for emergencies—medical, spiritual, monetary, cop-and-court, welfare.[4]
There are material and political benefits to be derived from having some of us working establishment jobs. But integration into the establishment bureaucracies is not woman's final answer. I do not think we can change the existing government, health, military, business or educational establishments significantly enough from within to bother with it. The internal structures of these institutions are designed to maintain a privileged elite and to organize even that elite in dominance-subordinance patterns. The health and welfare of women ultimately require entirely different ways of organizing things. If we were to try to transform the existing structures, our success would depend partly on enlightenment but largely on numbers. We would have to transcend tokenism. As long as a substantial majority of men are benefitting from the male-dominance within the institutions and in the world served by the institutions, and as long as men are in the substantial majority in these institutions, there is simply no reason why they should want, tolerate, or encourage enlightenment. The structures maintain the tokenism, which in turn protects the structures.

My conclusion, for now, is that a feminist can conscientiously hold and use an establishment position, *if* she is simultaneously cultivating skills, attitudes, identity and an alternative community, with and in which she can function without that position, and which will keep her honest while she has it. One day, when some who have been working straight jobs, and some have not, and all have been inventing new ways to survive and thrive, and when the evolving negotiations between my conscience and my patience set a new shit-limit which is found unacceptable by my employers; one day the time will be right for me to leave my post on the boundary and move into the new space.

1992 Postscript

It is clear enough that when I was writing the speech that became this essay, I was trying to come to grips with the phenomena of class and class privilege. Though I had come from a paradigm-case white middle class family background and education, feminism and lesbianism had brought me into a community of friends and associates that was both class-mixed and class-conscious. This essay documents the fact that U.S. feminism of the second wave was not, in its first decade, "a middle class phenomenon" in at least one sense—those articulating and developing it were not all middle class and were not oblivious to their class positions or the political importance of class. I was not oblivious, and members of the N.O.W. audience to whom I spoke at least were hearing about concerns about class privilege as it related to the liberation of women, however seriously they may or may not have taken it. Feminism and lesbian feminism of that period were in fact vehicles of increased class awareness (as of increased race awareness) for middle class white women. But also, as conscious and self-conscious as I was at that time about class, this essay reads to me in 1992 as strangely *un*conscious of class.

One thing that seems missing here is the balance of consciousness of myself as both class-privileged and *not* a member of the ruling class. My issue in 1976 was about whether or not to avail myself of certain opportunities. The existence and permanence of those opportunities seems to be utterly taken-for-granted. The essay seems to me now to betray no *working* consciousness of the fact that the those opportunities, that life, are not a permanent element of the natural order of the universe but a product of a certain phase in the processes of global capitalism. To the extent those processes are manipulable, they are manipulated by members of another class entirely than mine. Middle class privilege is not an immutable "given" and does not include the privilege of ruling and running the things that create and maintain the middle class and its privilege.[5]   In 1992 my academic job is still by world standards (and even by U.S. standards) plush and amazingly secure and the dollar amount of my present salary makes my reference in this essay to annual incomes of $15,000 seem comical. But "budget cuts" are coming down, teaching loads are going up; opportunities for interesting, creative, or innovative scholarly or instructional work are drying up; travel funds have disappeared almost entirely, and we have to supply our own paper, pencils, pens, printer ribbons; our use of the copying machine is strictly monitored, and we will not get cost-of-living raises (or "merit" raises) next year. My point is not "poor me"; I understand that I am still very well set in this world. My point is that the privileges of which I was going to avail myself (or not) are demonstrably mutable, contingent, dissolvable.

Also, in 1992 as I assemble this anthology many of my friends and acquaintances are unemployed or living with the daily threat of unemployment—both white collar and blue collar workers, and many have no medical insurance or may soon have none. It occurred to me within the last year, for the first time, that it might be irresponsible of me to give up the secure and well-paying job I have so chronically considered leaving, since we may well be coming into a period of economic desperation in which that income could be an invaluable *community* resource. Already some of my income is being worked into helping sustain some women more precariously, not to say desperately, situated than I, and it may become necessary for several or many women to live on this income. It is not only my own maintenance and survival (or that of my immediate kin) I must consider when I decide to avail myself or not to avail myself of these "middle class" opportunities (which are themselves not necessarily permanent), and it is not only the question of the contribution I can make to "the revolution"; survival issues within the community of my living are far closer to me (and really always have been) than I had any living, working idea of when I wrote "Who Wants a Piece of the Pie."

The author of "Who Wants a Piece of the Pie" was privileged to think of herself as born to a kind of security, autonomy, and control of her fate that in fact did not and do not exist for (middle class) her, if they exist for anybody. It may indeed be a "privilege" to live in such false consciousness, and I grieve the loss of it as though it were something valuable; but false, it is.

But the author of "Who Wants a Piece of the Pie" was, in my 1992 opinion, absolutely right about the matter of the kinds of personal and political investment a feminist might put into her job and place in a commercial, government, or educational institution and still maintain her integrity and radical edge. Though economic circumstances might make one stick with such a job when the negotiations of one's class/race/sex conscience would recommend quitting it, I think one yields everything up to the dominant order if one does not maintain a primary "homeplace" in a separate community of identity and value.[6]

¹ Published in *Quest: A Feminist Quarterly*, Vol.III, No.3, Winter, 1976-77, pp.28-35 and reprinted in *Building Feminist Theory: Essays from QUEST*, edited by the Quest Collective (New York, NY: Longman, 1981). This essay evolved from a lecture commissioned by NOW-Detroit for presentation in a series of lectures sponsored by them and funded by the Michigan Council for the Humanities. The lecture was delivered in Detroit, on May 19, 1976. I received much aid and advice from Carolyn Shafer in the thinking-through of these thoughts.

² This essay has a long history during which it has incorporated contributions by C. Rene Davis and by Carolyn Shafer who is, among other things, my regular thinking-partner. It got valuable criticism also from Jane English, Alison Jaggar, Sandra Harding and Adele Laslie. At this point in particular, this essay draws on conversations with Carolyn Shafer.

³ This paragraph draws on conversations with Rene Davis.

⁴ [In the original, there is a footnote at this point that recommends share-securing loans through your local feminist credit union as a way of sharing the benefits of financial solvency beyond the limits of one's own social circle. But in 1992, feminist credit unions are a thing of the past. In my community, though, and in other communities I know of, lesbians have organized to collect contributions and make grants anonymously, in order to accomplish that sort of sharing of resources. 1992]

⁵ Further thoughts on white middle class consciousness are worked out in my "Response to *Lesbian Ethics*" in this anthology.

⁶ Using her term "homeplace," I link my views with those of bell hooks. See "Homeplace," in *Yearning: Race, Gender, and Cultural Politics* (Boston: South End Press, 1990), pp. 41-49.

Not-Knowing About Sex and Power[1]
1980

Prologue

This essay is a critical response to a paper by philosopher Robert Ehman about "adult-child sex" given at a meeting of the Society for the Philosophy of Sex and Love, in April, 1980, in which he defended the view that such behavior is not necessarily harmful and should not be generally forbidden. That paper was considerably revised for publication in the anthology where it appeared with my "Critique." The published version is much more carefully argued and has a persuasive air of calm and sensible adult rationality, moderation, and good will about it that was lacking in the original version to which I first responded. The first version was more spontaneous and a bit sensational, and I think that it reflected more accurately the real carelessness of much "sex liberal" thinking. In the published paper Ehman in no way indicates that my criticism occasioned any revisions, but I suspect that it did. In that meeting, he and his friends seemed to find my criticism very severe and to think I was identifying him as a child-molester (a charge that on the strength of his own arguments he should have shrugged off as nothing to be concerned about). It does not much please me to think that my criticism enabled this author to clean up his act to look more respectable while the underlying failure to grasp the meanings of his issues for women and girls did not change a bit. This is a common sort of appropriation of feminist work which I try not to expose my work to. But sometimes it happens.

Here, then, is a summary *in Professor Ehman's lan-*

guage of the paper to which my essay is a response.

According to Ehman, there is an absolute and unquestioned prohibition on adult-child sex, a prohibition which needs special defense since philosophers have agreed that sexual acts *per se* are morally neutral. He admonishes his reader not to block the road to the rational inquiry that might contribute to moderating this prohibition.

Ehman says that the proscription against adult-child sex is the last bastion of sexual puritanism, and is supported now by two claims: (1) that adult-child sex is harmful to children; and (2) that children are incapable of valid consent to sex with adults.

Addressing the matter of harm, he surveys available research and concludes that there is no scientific proof of any substantial risk of harm to children, and what risk there is seems attached more to the existence of the proscription than to the sex itself. In the published version of his paper, Ehman acknowledges that a child is more vulnerable to intimidation and less able to lodge an effective complaint than an adult, and recommends a degree of paternalistic attention to adult-child sexual relationships to protect against abuse.

In the matter of consent, he argues that if children are incapable of rational informed consent, then consent is simply not an issue here, and the ground of argument can only return to the matter of harm.

###

Much of recent liberal moral philosophy about sex and the erotic is a great deal less valuable than it might have been because it originates in a distinctively male or male-identified perspective, serves interests associated with that perspective, and is deceptive on both of these scores. Professor Ehman's essay, "Adult-Child Sex," is a good example of this. It is worthwhile discussing the ways masculine values and perceptions dominate and distort this work, both because this sort of thing makes philosophers get things simply wrong and because such philosophy supports and encourages male dominance. It is also worthwhile to discuss this because the discussion may illuminate more generally distortions associated with privileged statuses of all sorts.

As is common in works of this genre, the primary

instrument of obfuscation is abstraction.

At the outset, Ehman invites us to share his assumption that "sex itself" is "morally neutral." Actually, we are not so much invited as required to accept this assumption, on pain of being counted among the "biased" and the "sexual puritans." So warm is the rhetoric of scorn that it seems clear that anyone who will not join in this fundamental assumption will be declared to be "blocking the road" of "rational inquiry." In effect, anyone who denies the assumption does not deserve classification as a philosopher and thus is not qualified for participation in the discourse at hand. This is rather a lot of force for an author to bring to bear in order to achieve agreement on something that supposedly is obvious and easily taken for granted.

This force is necessary, I think, not to pry the reader loose from cherished visions of the sexual innocence of childhood (which visions probably prompt disapproval of adult-child sex no more often than they fuel desires for it and for freedom from its prohibition), but to pry the reader's attention and sensibility loose from their moorings in rich experiential knowledge of the many and vivid meanings of sex. What Ehman is after is the detachment of cultural meanings from certain acts that he thinks can be contemplated "in themselves," as a prelude to critical assessment of the values attached to those acts in a particular culture. But what this act of intellectual artifice (a familiar one, to philosophers) accomplishes is detachment from all that informs and quickens moral and political intuition. To embrace such a dogma as "Sex itself is morally neutral" without caveat or qualification is to ignore all one has learned from childhood on about sexuality—sexuality as it is lived in this particular human culture. Whatever acts people engage in as "sex," the parties to them are invariably moving and feeling within a distinctive, complex medium of power, myth, value, and the deliberate manipulation of desire for commercial purposes. To usefully discuss questions about harm and benefit, consent and coercion, as they occur in that context, one has to map out and analyze the currents in this medium. These currents of cultural meaning connect those acts to connotations of domination and subordination, conquest and degradation, power and powerlessness, violence and victimization, as well as to pleasure or love. In this "semantics," dominance, conquest, power and violence are "marked" *masculine*. But to earn our stripes as liberals and rational inquirers, we are required to ignore all this.

This separation of moral philosophy from the grounds of moral intuition and political understanding sets the stage for the next move. If "sex itself" is morally neutral, then the only possible justification for any prohibition of any class of sexual acts or behavior must be in terms of the consequences of such acts in those sorts of cases. We must turn to the empirical matter of whether or not some degree of harm is risked by the act or behavior—some harm greater than that presumed to attend the prohibition of anything that is in itself morally neutral. The discussion of the "clinical literature" and the results of "controlled scientific research" that follow in Ehman's paper is remarkable on several scores.

Here is the vocabulary used to report the findings.[2] *The adjectives*: 'negative', 'better', 'less well', 'psychological', 'psychosexual', 'serious', 'severe', and 'seemingly normal'. *The nouns*: 'effect', 'impact', 'reaction', 'disturbance', 'problem', 'adjustment', 'maladjustment', 'psychosis', 'functioning'. Pseudoscientific psychobabble. The most meaningful terms used are 'guilt', 'self-esteem', 'nightmare', 'compulsive bathing', 'crying', and 'bedwetting'. Surely it is no surprise that the literature soberly seeking correlations between "psychosexual adjustments" or "psychological disturbances" on the one hand and certain events characterized as "sexual experiences" or "sexual contacts" (conceived as themselves bare of moral meaning) on the other, is inconclusive. With vocabulary as empirically void as this, one can show nothing; but one can appear to show whatever one wishes. What does surprise me is that the vacuousness of this literature is claimed by Ehman to justify skepticism in the matter of what harm adult-child sex might do the child, skepticism tilted a bit in favor of "serious doubt" as to whether there is "a substantial risk of harm." Such literature leaves doubt because it is almost totally meaningless, not because it reveals any empirical truth or verifies any empirical hypotheses. The retreat to this literature leaves us empty-handed, but it also brings in a false posture of empty-handedness assumed in the interest of something like "objectivity." The discipline of "rational inquiry" is presumed to require that we pretend to be ignorant of what we know, as the only way to avoid being helplessly in the sway of prejudice—of traditional, uncriticized, conservative cultural values to which we are attached by training, habit, and emotion.

But we are not ignorant. We all—women, men, girls, and boys of various cultures and classes—know a good deal about sex and sexuality as they are experienced by persons holding and being held, kissing and being kissed, encountering one's own or another's nudity, fondling and being fondled, fucking and being fucked, when any of these is novel or strange, or when it is familiar; and what it is like to like it or loathe it, to be transported to ecstacy or to dissociation, lying or telling the truth, being lied to or being told the truth, understanding or being bewildered, or any of these things in any combination. In the name of intellectual integrity we are supposed to pretend we know nothing of all this and therefore have nothing upon which to ground reasonable judgments about how it is or would likely be for a child, in this or that sort of situation, to be involved in sexual activity or in a sexual relationship with an adult who holds this or that social position relative to the child; we are required to rest our moral philosophizing instead upon a handful of studies—in fact, in the present case, on just one study.[3] Ehman judges it to be scientifically rigorous; it is apparently the only one his search turned up that even pretends to such merit, though we are given no reason to believe that it has been replicated.

We do not, to be sure, know all the same things about all this, and neither conservative nor liberal orthodoxies take much account of what women know. Liberal arguments generally favor extensions of the range of permitted or accepted sex, and they generally take it for granted that sex itself is a good. (This contradicts the first dogma, that sex itself is morally neutral; but that would not defeat the claim that these are both dogmas of a single orthodoxy.) To play the game of liberal moral philosophy, one is expected to assume that in the absence of coercion, force, exploitation, and the contaminations due to superstitious or puritanical prohibitions, sex is to be entered under the "benefits" column in one's utilitarian bookkeeping, as Ehman enters it in his analogies with pharmaceuticals and pollutions. His exposition proceeds as though in cases where sex is "harmless" it can be assumed to be "pleasurable or loving" or "satisfying." There is much evidence, recorded and cited in such sources as the Kinsey and Hite reports, commonplace in woman-only conversation, and revealed by background assumptions in such books as *The Total Woman,* that sex itself is often found by a large number of its participants to be alienating and boring, or worse. Many women often find that even where they are not coerced or forced, where they enter the encounter with clear and guiltless erotic desire, sex itself does not bring on orgasm or give satisfaction, not to mention ecstasy or any other of the more pyrotechnic "benefits." In a world in which many people, even if not a majority, find that sex itself is something they would cheerfully do without, and would desire sex only if it is accompanied by other things, like intimacy, personal affection, equality of presence, reciprocity of attention, and so forth, one cannot in good conscience accept as a given and a universal that if only there is not force, coercion or exploitation, sex is something whose prohibition deprives people of a benefit.

The discussion of harm, in Ehman's essay, focusses both on factors that would make a sexual contact a sexual assault and on consequences. If we are convinced that no physical damage is done, that the child is willing and that "science" can be construed as assuring that there is little risk of bad consequences, then there are no further questions; regarding cases that meet these standards there can be no justification for a general prohibition, social or legal. But I would have more questions: How was it for her? Not: Did this, or is it likely to, result in lifelong psychosexual dysfunction? but: Was it nice? Did she have fun? Was it not soured by ambivalence, confusion, pain, feelings of powerlessness, anxiety about displeasing a partner on whom she is emotionally and materially dependent, fear of pregnancy? And if it is not good, can she, will she, would she dare, make this clear to him? Any woman with reasonably broad sexual experience knows the meanings of these questions. Ehman's discussion of the question of what harm might be done by adult-child sex removes attention and sensibility from the experience itself. An experience can be horrible without precipitating bedwetting or causing "maladjustment." Are we to say it is harmless if it is merely wretched but does not demonstrably cause behavior that parents or clinical psychologists identify as "problematic?"

Ehman would have us philosophize about sex without taking into account either sexual politics or the knowledge of sexual experience that we have first-hand and by way of literature, conversation, and research. When we take all this into account, *power* and *gender* move into the center of the moral picture. In fact, our attention has been misdirected from the beginning by the use of the phrase "adult-child sex." This gender-washing term diverts our attention from the question of which adults show an interest in sex with which children.

Court records indicate that in the neighborhood of 95 percent or more of adults engaging in sex with children are males, and in the neighborhood of 87 to 90 percent of the children are females. The practice of adult-child sex is gendered. Furthermore, such records indicate that most of the cases involve the child's social or biological father. One survey found that 90 percent of the cases of adult-child sex were father-daughter, stepfather-stepdaughter, or grandfather-granddaughter, and that of the remaining 10 percent, half were father-son.[4] It has everything to do with gender and the power of the male, the patriarch.

Though some people may indeed object to adult-child sex because they see it as defiling an imagined childhood innocence, many who approach the question from the life experience of a woman in phallocratic (male-dominated, male-governed, male-protecting) culture are alarmed, not by visions of sullied childhood innocence, but by the enormity of the power-imbalance that obtains in such relationships. As long as the culture is male-dominated, misogynist, and characterized by compulsory heterosexuality for women, most females will have most of their sexual experience in relationships in which, on balance, they have considerably less social, economic, and physical power than their partners and in a context of myth and dogma that would impose male-affirming and female-degrading meanings upon their sexual acts and contacts. That is bad enough, without the addition of the power-imbalance of the adult-child nexus in a culture with little respect for children and the power-imbalance of the father-daughter nexus in a culture in which generally there is much confusion of *father* and *god*. Intellectually and emotionally mature, financially independent adult women have enough trouble knowing their own minds and bodies and defending their pleasure and their integrity in the coercive context of power imbalance that they move in as sexual beings; that a person who is totally dependent materially, in the process of socialization to femininity, and operating with a child's emotional and intellectual resources could do so in the even more coercive context of the father-daughter connection is utterly implausible.[5]

When men explore in imagination (however carefully and with whatever critical sensitivity) the acts and circumstances of sex or sexual relationship between a man and a girl, their situation as men in this society puts them at a double disadvantage for appreciating the dangers for the girl. The experience of men has been almost wholly that of the person in the position of greater power, and it is one of the more dubious privileges of power that it can easily fail to know itself; and then, not knowing one's own power, one also cannot see how the power itself interferes with one's knowing the less powerful other.

As a student's professor, with the power of grades and letters of reference, you ask that student (who is going by the department anyway) to drop something off at the department for you. Though at some level you are of course cognizant of the fact that professors have power with respect to students, you certainly do not feel that you are pressuring this student. After all, you did not threaten to lower the student's grade for refusal to do this small favor, and anyway, you are not that sort and the student ought to know you well enough to know that. But you, unlike, say, the student's roommate, are so positioned, willy-nilly, that if you come to the view that this student is a rather cold or unfriendly person who does not like you much, you could read her/his papers less sympathetically and recommend her/him less warmly, and thus penalize the student for her/his unwillingness to respond to your request with generosity or friendliness. To her/his roommate the student can say, "Drop off your own book; I'm not your servant!" One does not say that to one's professor, whether or not one likes, respects, or feels used by one's professor. That you think you do not allow your feelings about students and theirs about you to affect your grades or recommendations just has no weight in the student's situation; what has weight is the fact that you could—you have that power. Savvy students behave in a generous and friendly way with professors; cruder ones flatter; they are looking after themselves in a coercive situation. Junior professors do the same with department chairpersons. The latter cannot issue a dinner invitation without the former being under some pressure (it can be pressure without being great or irresistible pressure) to accept, and to accept in a manner that indicates an expectation of enjoying the evening. If the chairperson thinks she/he and her/his spouse are witty conversationalists and good cooks, the junior professor is unlikely to challenge this conceit.

If the father thinks he is a sensitive and skillful lover, the daughter he is honoring with his sexual attentions is unlikely to tell him otherwise.

I and many other people I regularly encounter tend to think of ourselves as good-willed, benevolent, intelligent, and perceptive, and those over whom we have power have every motive to play to our good opinions of ourselves. The structure of power mitigates systematically against those others being honest with us about anything that would displease us, and to the extent that one's power takes the form of authority, the structure mitigates even against their being honestly knowledgeable of themselves, since they will not only try to act in ways that avoid displeasing us but may even to some extent accept our authority as to what they are, what they are thinking, and how they feel. The more power one has, the more impenetrable are these barriers.

Being in a position of power in a situation not only mitigates against one's having good access to knowledge of the other's wishes and attitudes and the quality of the other's experience, it also tends to make one think precisely that one does know what is going on. One's power gives one the feeling of being in control of this situation—that one can make it be what one wants it to be. So if one has good intentions, and means to take care not to harm the other, means to arrange for the other a pleasant, instructive, and satisfying experience, one expects both to be able to do it and to know one has done it. The same power one thinks can be neutralized by one's good will, one expects to use to make the situation and experience a good one.

It is a matter of the structures of power; fathers are in no position to take good care of daughters with whom they are sexually involved, and their daughters are in no position to take care of themselves. There are like problems, even if they are not so heavily over-determined, in any adult-child sexual encounter or relationship, and indeed such structures have to be negotiated in any situation of sex between people who are unequal in power.

M y own inclinations are anarchistic enough to make me disinclined to argue for criminalization of this or that sort of sexual act, or acts with this or that partner, though in cases of adult-child sex where the adult is totally outside the net of the child's family, the legal prohibition might give the child just the leverage she/he needs to equalize the power in the relationship. But I am inclined to favor social pressure against sexual acts and relationships in any case of marked difference of social and economic power between the parties. (For this principle not to rule out heterosexual relations between adults, perhaps we should have to bring about the feminist revolution. If so, so be it.) The less the difference of age and physical size, the less the difference of power the participants have with others in the surrounding situation, and in the absence of one party's material dependence on the other, the less reason there would be to enjoin children's sexual activity. Perhaps if they experience sexuality between equals in childhood they will have the strength and good sense to refuse anything less in adulthood.

At this point, a "sex-liberal" would ask, and rightly so, why this should apply to sex and not to all sorts of adult-child activity and interaction. My answer has to do with what sex is *in a culture of the sort we are living in.* Sex, unlike baking cookies, going camping, or playing catch, engages some of our strongest emotions and most desperate needs in an enterprise powerfully associated with dominance and subordination, violence and victimization, a mythology of ladies and whores, queers and Real Men, ideas of "dirt" and "filth," and so on and on; and though it might be otherwise in some other human culture, in this culture, if there is one situation in which people cannot perceive others, are least able to perceive others' interests as disparate from their own, it is when they are in the sway of erotic desire, when they are in lust. There may indeed be other things besides sex that we should discourage adults from doing with children, such as taking them hunting; and perhaps fathers should not have control of their children's financial resources, so the whole matter of material provision is removed from the politically sticky relationship of the child with its father.

The sexual access of males to females is an absolutely central matter to male supremacy, to masculine identity, and to competition and aggression among men. Men rape "each other's" women in war and in feuds, they prove their masculinity through copulation, they maintain control of women by rape. (These things are true in a great many cultures and times.) In a culture such as this, I cannot, myself, shake off my cynicism in the face of any new effort to expand the range of men's sexual access to females. What is gained, and for whom, by putting aside the suspicions rooted in our experience and knowledge of sex and sexual politics, and reasoning airily about "sex itself" between (genderless, positionless) "adults" and "children"? Such philosophy only encourages all of the ignorance that the more powerful have of their power and as a result of their power. What encourages this ignorance also encourages the maintenance of the system that gives them that power. Not-knowing is the best insurance against the guilty conscience that might make one uncomfortable in one's privileges.

[1] This paper was published under the title, "Critique," as a reply to a paper by Robert Ehman entitled, "Adult-Child Sex," in *Philosophy and Sex*, 2nd edition, editors, Robert Baker and Frederick Elliston (NY: Prometheus Books, 1984).

[2] What follows here refers to the text of the paper Ehman read, which differs from the published version. The published version agrees with the earlier version in coming to the conclusion that there was at the time not much clinical or "scientific" information available about harm to children from sexual contact with adults, and most of it was inconclusive. Much more literature is available in 1992 documenting the harm done to children by sexual contacts and assaults by adults. See the Bibliography following.

[3] [Ehman requires this discipline of ignorance in service of a modern sort of "rationality" and "objectivity"; some postmodern critics of feminism seem to require a like discipline of ignorance in order to avoid uses of terms like 'man' and 'woman' and 'woman's experience' which they say are essentialist. 1992]

[4] [Various sources and modes of study generate various statistics, and a great deal more information is now available than was in 1980 when this was written. See the Bibliography on p.49 for references which will lead the researcher to full and current information on the incidence of child sexual assault. 1992]

[5] [Rich collections of women's own narratives of their experience of father-daughter incest are now available. See the Bibliography on p.49.1992]

Bibliography

Armstrong, Louise. *Kiss Daddy Goodnight: A Speak-out on Incest.* New York: Hawthorn Books, 1978.

Bass, Ellen. *The Courage To Heal: A Guide for Women Survivors of Child Sexual Abuse.* New York: Harper & Row, 1988.

Butler, Sandra. *Conspiracy of Silence: the Trauma of Incest.* San Francisco: New Glide Publications, 1978.

Janssen, Martha. *Silent Scream.* Philadelphia: Fortress Press, 1983.

McNaron, Toni A.H., and Yarrow Morgan, eds. *Voices in the Night: Women Speaking about Incest.* Minneapolis, Minn.: Cleis Press, 1982.

Russell, Diana E. H. *The Secret Trauma: Incest in the Lives of Girls and Women.* New York: Basic Books, 1986.

Ward, Elizabeth. *Father-Daughter Rape.* London: Women's Press, 1984.

A Lesbian's Perspective on Women's Studies[1]

1980

Looking at women's studies from my Lesbian perspective and with my Lesbian feminist sensibility, what I see is that women's studies is heterosexual. The predominance of heterosexual perspectives, values, commitments, thought and vision is usually so complete and ubiquitous that it cannot be perceived, for lack of contrast. (Like the air on a calm and moderate day; the way sexism still is for many people.) Sometimes, usually because of the interruption and contrast imported by my own presence, the basically and pervasively heterosexual character of women's studies is very clear and perceptible—overwhelming and deeply disappointing. It is also, usually, unspoken and unspeakable.

Some of my colleagues in women's studies say they cannot really tell the truth or "be radical" in their teaching because it would alienate the students. I tell them not to worry about alienating people; I say that the truth is challenging, interesting, compelling and very effective in the classroom. I also say that when one attempts just to tell the truth, the responses, whether constructive or hostile, honest or dishonest, will be the best clues to one's errors. But in my dealings with my heterosexual women's studies colleagues, I do not take my own advice: I have routinely and habitually muffled or stifled myself on the subject of Lesbianism and heterosexualism, feminism and women's studies, out of some sort of concern about alienating them. Some of these women are tangibly peculiar about Lesbianism and are already offended by my being uncloseted and blatant; I do not think they have noticed that I avoid discussing Lesbianism and heterosexuality with them for fear their already nervous association with women's studies would become simply untenable for them. Much more important to me is a smaller number who are my dependable political co-workers in the university, the ones in the academic world with clearest and strongest feminist and anti-racist politics, the ones with some commitment to not being homophobic and to trying to be comprehending and supportive of Lesbians and Lesbianism. If I estrange these women, I will lose the only footing I have politically and personally, in my long-term work-a-day survival in academia. They are important, valuable and respected allies. I am very careful, over-careful, when I talk about heterosexuality with them.

But the situation is asymmetrical, as it always is with minority or marginal people and majority or dominant people. What is *a topic* for them, which some can and some cannot attend to fruitfully, is a condition of life for me. I avoid "alienating" them, but they constantly and (usually) unconsciously alienate me by their mostly uncritical and apparently unalterable, to me un- fathomable, commitment to heterosexuality—by which I mean deeply bound emotional and intellectual commitments to men, to reform, to integration and to the centrality and natural necessity of heterosexual genital sex. The unwelcome weight of this heterosexualism is a salient fact of my life, and its manifestations in the politics of women's studies are coming very clear to me and should be stated.

In my experience with women's studies it seems common and characteristic for the women instructors to assume that widespread heterosexuality and the dominance of heterosexual conceptions have always been and will always be The Way It Is for humans on this planet, in particular, for women on this planet. Lesbianism is seen by most of them (but not all) as an acceptable, plausible alterative for some women and is understood (not by all) at least at a verbal level to be clearly coherent with feminism. But they all believe that it is only realistic to understand that most women are and most women will be heterosexual, at least for the duration of any era that our practical politics can concern itself with. Women's studies programming is grounded on the assumption that the vast majority of the students are and always will be heterosexual. Hence we give them almost entirely heterosexual women's literature, the history of heterosexual women,[2] and analysis of the roles of

heterosexual women in work, business, the arts and heterosexual domestic life. It is also assumed that we should support
(not just tolerate) speakers, films, workshops, classes, whole
courses, which encourage women to prepare themselves to cope
with life in the "dual career marriage," teach how to be married
and a feminist, and train them in the tricks of legislative reform
so they can try to ensure that abortions will be available to them
when they need them, since they obviously will not practice the
only safe and sure method of contraception.[3] We presume the
students are hopelessly heterosexual and cater to the interests
and needs we assume heterosexual women to have, instead of
assuming they are educable to other ways of living, different
needs and interests, and some non- or anti-heterosexist sensibility and politics.

Women's studies, as an institution, as I know it, actively
and aggressively supports women in becoming and remaining
heterosexual; it actively seeks to encourage women to believe
that the personal, political, economic and health problems associated with heterosexuality for women should be struggled with
rather than avoided—that these problems are inevitable but
more-or-less solvable (with great endurance and much work),
rather than that they are unsolvable but definitely evitable.

I am notorious in my town for my recruitment of women
to Lesbianism and Lesbian perspectives. But what I do is minus-
cule. Imagine a real reversal of the heterosexualist teaching our
program provides. Imagine thirty faculty members at a large
university engaged routinely and seriously in the vigorous and
aggressive encouragement of women to be Lesbians, helping
them learn skills and ideas for living as Lesbians, teaching the
connections between Lesbianism and feminism and between
heterosexism and sexism, building understanding of the agency
of individual men in keeping individual women in line for the
patriarchy. Imagine us openly and actively advising women not
to marry, not to fuck, not to become bonded with any man.
Imagine us teaching *lots* of Lesbian literature, poetry, history
and art in women's studies courses, and teaching out of a politics
determined by Lesbian perception and sensibility. Imagine all
this going on as actively and openly and enthusiastically as the
program now promotes the searching out of careers and "feminist men," the development of "egalitarian marriages" and the
management of heterosexual sex and the family.[4]

But the politics which women's studies purveys, even when some material by or about Lesbians is included in some courses, is heterosexual politics. And according to heterosexual politics, Lesbianism could never be the norm, and promoting Lesbianism for women generally is somewhere between unrealistic and abusive.

The people who are the primary agents in determining and promoting this politics in women's studies are the heterosexual feminists in academia. These women are (not without exception) quite good in their relations with the few Lesbians they work with—supportive, tolerant, useful. But this friendly, open-minded, even appreciative attitude camouflages their continuing and firm commitment to our marginality. Their being friendly and supportive and respectful to a few Lesbians (who inevitably serve as tokens) has obscured from me and from them the enduring fact that they never take seriously any idea that Lesbians and Lesbianism *should not be marginal.*

I want to ask heterosexual academic feminists to do some hard analytical and reflective work. To begin, I want to say to them:

I wish you would notice that you are heterosexual.
I wish you would grow to the understanding that you choose *heterosexuality.*

I would like you to rise each morning and know that you are heterosexual and that you choose to be heterosexual— that you are and choose to be a member of a privileged and dominant class, one of your privileges being not to notice.

I wish you would stop and seriously consider, as a broad and long-term feminist political strategy, the conversion of women to a woman-identified and woman-directed sexuality and eroticism, as a way of breaking the grip of men on women's minds and women's bodies, of removing women from the chronic attachment to the primary situations of sexual and physical violence that is rained upon women by men, and as a way of promoting women's firm and reliable bonding against oppression.

Some heterosexual women have said in response to these sorts of sayings, "I see the connection between Lesbianism and feminism, but I cannot just decide to be a Lesbian...I'm not sexually attracted to women: women just don't turn me on." And I want to ask, "Why not? Why don't women turn you on? Why aren't you attracted to women?" I do not mean these questions rhetorically. I am completely serious.

The suppression of Lesbian feeling, sensibility and response has been so thorough and so brutal for such a long time, that if there were not a strong and widespread inclination to Lesbianism, it would have been erased from human life. There is so much pressure on women to be heterosexual, and this pressure is both so pervasive and so completely denied, that I think heterosexuality cannot come naturally to many women: I think that widespread heterosexuality among women is a highly artificial product of the patriarchy. I suspect that it is not true at all that we must assume that most women are and most women will forever be heterosexual. I think that most women have to be coerced into heterosexuality. I would like heterosexual women to consider this proposition, *seriously*. I want heterosexual women to do intense and serious consciousness-raising and exploration of their own personal histories and to find out how and when in their own development the separation of women from the erotic came about for them.[5] I would like heterosexual women to be as actively curious about how and why and when they became heterosexual as I have been about how and why and when I became Lesbian.

At this point it might seem that I am demanding of heterosexual women their respect for my choice but that I am unwilling to respect theirs. I think, though, that it is respectful of autonomy to genuinely inquire into the history and grounds of choices, and disrespectful or negligent of autonomy to let unfreedom masquerade as choice or let the declaration "It's my choice" close off rather than open up inquiry.

Millions of heterosexual women give no thought to what heterosexuality is or why they are heterosexual. Heterosexuality is understood by them to *be* sexuality, and they assume uncritically and unthinkingly that it is simply the way humans are; they do not perceive heterosexuality as *an* option. Where there are no perceived options, there can be no such thing as choice, and hence one cannot respect the choice. But well-educated, worldly, politically astute, thoughtful, analytical, feminist women do know perfectly well that there are options, and that Lesbian life is an option that coheres very well with feminist politics. They do choose to be heterosexual. Respect for that choice (on my part and on their part) demands that they make that choice intelligible.

Many feminist Lesbians have thought and reflected and written and worked very hard to demonstrate that our choice makes sense. We have gone forth and participated on panels and in workshops, and appeared on television explaining ourselves. We have, over and over, at great personal risk and considerable cost, worked as hard as we knew how to make our choice intelligible to audiences ranging from the idle curious to the skeptical to the openly hostile. Respect for heterosexuals' choice demands equally that they show, within the gentle standards of rationality recommended by womanly sensibility, that their choice can be understood as a *reasonable choice*. Until this has been shown I will not grant the assumption that heterosexuality can make sense for feminists, and I am not willing to continue uncritical acceptance of women's studies programs promoting heterosexuality for women.

Unless many heterosexual feminists start working as hard at making their choice intelligible as Lesbians have worked at making ours intelligible, they should refrain from teaching and publishing and other work which openly or implicitly encourages other women in becoming or remaining committed to heterosexuality, and Lesbians should refrain from supporting women's studies.

1992 Postscript

I gave the transcript of this talk to my heterosexual women friends in Women's Studies at my home institution, and they discussed it among themselves. The reports that came back to me indicated to me that they were (understandably) discomfitted by the anger in this talk and tended to respond somewhat defensively. But apparently it did stimulate some of them to discuss their sexuality together in different ways than they had before. Apparently they thought there was a contradiction in my argument, where I was simultaneously saying their heterosexuality was a choice and saying that there was a history of their becoming heterosexual, a history of the separation of women from the erotic for them, and that there is great pressure on women to be heterosexual. That does not seem like a contradiction to me. I did not mean that one can just choose, all of a sudden and for doctrinal reasons, to be aroused by different things than what has aroused one up to now. But one can choose environments to place oneself in, one can choose literature to read and art to engage with, one can choose to think critically about things one has not thought critically about before, and one can choose also how one presents oneself in the world. As canny consumers, we choose, for instance, to mute the TV when ads come on, to read more and watch TV less, to engage more with people who resist consumerism and less with people who are into it, and as persons concerned to take care intelligently of our health, we wean ourselves from foods we are more or less addicted to and regularly crave by exposing ourselves to selected information and images, engaging more with others who model good eating and less with others who model poor eating, by willfully changing some of our behavior so it is out of line with the desires we want to unlearn and in line with desire we want to learn. And in time, we actually do alter our desires, wishes, needs, patterns of excitement and so on. It may be that it would not be wise for a heterosexual woman to engage in retraining her erotic desires; it may be that it would be wise. But the fact that those desires have a history and that history includes coercive pressure does not mean she does not have many choices to make with respect to those desires. At the time I was composing this talk, I thought that many of the heterosexual women I encountered in Women's Studies had chosen to view those desires as natural, given, inborn, immutable, and had chosen to live them out to a great extent in accord with the patterns of female heterosexuality as it is institutionalized in contemporary patriarchy.

The practical question that this speech gives rise to is that of whether this angry lesbian continued to engage in Women's Studies. She did, and she still does. I have, after all, not been willing to hand Women's Studies over to heterosexualism. In spite of everything, Lesbians and lesbian meaning can be sheltered and nurtured in Women's Studies programs, and the influence of Lesbians on Women's Studies has been significant and salutary. Politically, Women's Studies is a far more suitable home in the academy than is the newly developing and euphemistically named "Lesbian and Gay Studies," where lesbians have to struggle almost from scratch for feminist analyses and feminist perspectives, as well as against the sexist perceptions and behavior of the men involved.[6]

Tension and anger between lesbian and non-lesbian feminists in the academy still exists and still surfaces from time to time, and very basic questions about sexuality and feminist politics are still utterly and painfully unresolved. My own most recent effort to come to grips with some of it is in "Willful Virgin *or* Do You Have To Be A Lesbian To Be A Feminist?" in this anthology.

[1] This essay is a slightly revised version of a talk I gave at the 1980 conference of the National Women's Studies Association on a panel titled "Lesbian Perspectives on Women's Studies," organized by Sarah Hoagland. My thoughts reflect discussions with my lover Carolyn Shafer, and she gave help and suggestions in the revision process. The essay was published under the title "Assignment: NWSA-Bloomington-1980: Speak on 'Lesbian Perspectives on Women's Studies'" in *Sinister Wisdom*, 14, Fall 1980, pp. 3-7, was reprinted with the title "Lesbian Perspectives on Women's Studies" in *Lesbian Studies*, edited by Margaret Cruickshank (Old Westbury, NY: The Feminist Press, 1982), and in German translation in *Women's Studies An Den Hochschulen Der USA: Americanische Frauen Sprechen*, edited by Renate Duelli-Klein and Maresi Nerad, in the series *Blickpunkt Hochschuldidaktik* printed and distributed by Arbeitsgemeinschaft fuer Hochschuldidaktik.

[2] ...or the literature and history of women *presumed* to be heterosexual. The evidence that many of the women we study were Lesbians is generally overlooked—an erasure that builds in added security for the assumption of natural near-universal heterosexuality.

[3] By "the only safe and sure method," I do not mean only exclusive Lesbianism, but whatever would add up to total female control of reproductive sexual intercourse.

[4] For a sense of the magnitude of this, consider: at Michigan State the women's studies classes account for well over 12,000 student-credit-hours each year.

[5] This phrase is due to Adrienne Rich. My thought on these things have benefitted from my correspondence with her.

[6] See Marilyn Frye, "Lesbian Feminism and the Gay Rights Movement: Another View of Male Supremacy, Another Separatism," in *The Politics of Reality* (Freedom, CA: The Crossing Press, 1983).

The Possibility of
Feminist Theory[1]
1990

Imagine that a single individual had written up an exhaustive description of a sedated elephant as observed from one spot for one hour and then, with delighted self-satisfaction, had heralded that achievement as a complete, accurate and profound account of The Elephant. The androcentrism of the accumulated philosophy and science of the "western" world is like that. A few, a few men, have with a like satisfaction told the story of the world and human experience—have created what pretends to be progressively a more and more complete, accurate and profound account of what they call "Man and His World." The *Man* whose (incomplete) story this is turns out to be a species of males to which there is awkwardly, problematically and paradoxically appended a subspecies or alterspecies of individuals which men are born of but which are not men. It is, to put it mildly, a story which does not fit women and which women do not fit.

In the light of what is generally considered common knowledge (i.e., the official story of "Man and His World") a great deal of most women's experience appears anomalous, discrepant, idiosyncratic, chaotic, "crazy."[2]   In that dim light our lives are to a great extent either unintelligible or intelligible only as pathological or degenerate. As long as each woman thinks that her experience alone is thus discrepant, she tends to trust the received wisdom and distrust her own senses and judgment. For instance, she will believe that her "inexplicable" pain is imaginary, a phantasm. It is in the consciousness-raising conversations among women (however intentionally or unintentionally joined) that women discover that similar "anomalies" occur in most of their lives and that those "anomalies" taken together form a pattern, or many patterns. The fragments which were each woman's singular oddities (often previously perceived as her own faults or defects) are collectively perceived to fit together into a coherent whole. The happy side of this is that we learn we are not sick or monstrous and we learn to trust our perception. The unhappy side is that the coherent whole we discover is a pattern of oppression. Women's lives are full and overflowing with the evidence of the imbalanced distribution of woes and wealth as between the women and the men of each class, race and circumstance. In consciousness-raising the data coalesces into knowledge: knowledge of the oppression of women by men.

When women's experience is made intelligible in the communications of consciousness-raising we can recognize that it is in the structures of men's stories of the world that women don't make sense—that our own experience, collectively and jointly appreciated, can generate a picture of ourselves and the world within which we are intelligible. The consciousness-raising process reveals us to ourselves as authoritative perceivers which are neither men nor the fantastical, impossible feminine beings which populate the men's world-story. Our existence is not inherently paradoxical or problematic. Our existence *is* an indigestible mass of discrepant data for the patriarchal world-story. From the point of view of the discrepant data, that story appears appallingly partial and distorted—it seems a childish and fantastic, albeit dangerous, fiction. Assuming our perceptual authority, we have undertaken, as we must, to re-write the world. The project of feminist theory is to write a new Encylopaedia. It's title: *The World, According to Women*.[3]

The historically dominant "western" man-made world-story claims universality and objectivity but, from the point of view of feminists, conspicuously lacks both. Thinking to improve upon that story, we assumed ours should be both. By adding voices to the conversation, we expected we would achieve a broader consensus in the intersubjective agreement that justifies the claim to objectivity, and thus also a grounding for legitimate universalization.[4]

As most introductory philosophy textbooks will tell you, the "western" tradition of philosophy presupposes the intelligibility of the universe—the doctrine the *it* and *we* (human beings) are such that it can be understood by us. The human knower, in principle any human knower, can, in principle, understand the universe.[5] This presupposes a fundamental uniformity of human knowers such that in principle any knower is interchangeable with any other knower. In practice it means that as you add to the group whose intersubjective agreement will count as objectivity, you are adding pieces of a single and coherent cosmic jigsaw puzzle. You may not know where the pieces fit, but you presume it is not possible that any of them do not fit. Non-congruence of observers' observations either is merely apparent or is due to observers' mistakes or errors which are themselves ultimately explainable, ultimately congruent with the rest of the world-picture. Buying this body of doctrine, one thinks all knowers are essentially alike, that is, are essentially like oneself; one thinks then that one can speak not just as oneself, but as a human being.

For feminist thinkers of the present era the first and most fundamental act of our own emancipation was granting ourselves authority as perceivers, and we accomplished that act by discovering agreement in the experiences and perceptions of women. It makes sense that when the feminist thinker assumes her authority as a knower, she would claim her equal perceptual rights in the pseudo-democracy of the interchangeable knowers of the intelligible universe. It makes sense that she would carry over the assumption that all knowers are essentially alike into the supposition that all humans similarly positioned (in this case, as women in patriarchy) have in principle, as knowers, the same knowledge. She would think she could speak not just as herself but as a woman.

The new world-writers had first to overcome the deceptions and distortions which made us unknown to ourselves. We have made remarkable progress: many, many of us have rewritten many chapters of our own lives and are living lives neither we nor our mothers would have imagined possible, or even imagined at all. We have deconstructed canons, re-periodized history, revised language, dissolved disciplines, added a huge cast of characters and broken most of the rules of logic and good taste. But we have also discovered our own vast ignorance of other women of our own time. We have repeatedly discovered that we have overlooked or misunderstood the truths of the experience of some groups of women and that we have ourselves been overlooked or misunderstood by some other segment or school of feminist thought. We have had great difficulty coming to terms with the fact of differences among women—differences associated with race, class, ethnicity, religion, nationality, sexuality, age, physical ability and even such variety among women as is associated just with peculiarities of individual personal history.

What we want to do is to speak of and to and from the circumstances, experience and perception of those who are historically, materially, culturally constructed by or through the concept *woman*. But the differences among women across cultures, locales and generations make it clear that although all female humans may live lives shaped by concepts of Woman, they are not all shaped by the same concept of Woman. Even in any one narrowly circumscribed community and time, no female individual is a rubber stamp replica of the prevailing concept of Woman. (In the case of the concept of Woman that prevails in my neighborhood, the concept itself is internally contradictory; nobody *could* fit it.) Furthermore, Woman is not the only concept or social category any of us lives under. Each of us is a woman of some class, some color, some occupation, some ethnic or religious group, and one is or is not someone's sister, wife, mother, daughter, aunt, teacher, student, boss or employee. One is, or is not, alcoholic, a survivor of cancer, a survivor of the Holocaust. One is or is not able-bodied. One is fat or thin. One is lesbian or heterosexual or bisexual or off-scale. A woman of color moves in the ("western") world as both "a woman" and "of color." A white woman also moves both as woman and as white, whether or not her experience forces upon her a clear consciousness of the latter. Lesbians must reject the question: are you more fundamentally women, or lesbians? And we insist that heterosexual women recognize that everywhere they move as women they also move as heterosexual. No one encounters the world simply as *a woman*. Nobody observes and theorizes simply as *a woman*. If there are in every locale perspectives and meanings which can properly be called women's, there is nonetheless no such thing as *a* or *the* woman's story of what is going on.

Schematically, and experientially, The Problem of Difference in Feminist Theory is simple: A good deal of feminist thinking has issued in statements and descriptions that pertain to "women," and are not modified to mark distinctions among women. And these are the sorts of statements their authors want to be making. But when such statements and descriptions are delivered in public they meet up with critics, who are women, who report that the statements are appallingly partial, untrue or even unintelligible when judged by those women's own experience and by what is common knowledge among women of their kind, class or group. This criticism seems to be (and I have felt it to be), simply, devastating.

Feminism (the worldview, the philosophy) rests on a most empirical base, namely, staking your life on the trustworthiness of your own body as a source of knowledge. It rests equally fundamentally on intersubjective agreement, since it is some kind of agreement in perceptions and experience among women which gives our sense-data, our body-data, the compelling cogency which made it possible to trust it. It is an unforgettable, irreversible and definitive fact of feminist experience that respect for women's experience/voice/perception/knowledge, our own and others', is the ground and foundation of our emancipation—of both the necessity and the possibility of rewriting, recreating, the world. Thus it is only by a violent dishonesty that we could, or can, fail to give credence to women's voices even when they wildly differ and conflict. And when we do give them credence it soon becomes clear that taken as a whole, "women's experience" is not uniform and coherent in the ways required to ground a structure of knowledge, as that would traditionally be understood.[6]

Thus has the feminist faith in and respect for the experience and voice of every woman seemed to lead us into the valley of the shadow of Humanism—wishywashy, laissez-faire, I'mOK-You'reOK, relativistic humanism (or seemed more recently to lead us into the bottomless bog of relativistic apolitical postmodernism) where there are no Women and there is no Truth. Which is not where we want to be.

The way out, or the way back in, I think, is to get clearer about how the practice of feminist theory departed from the predominating modern "western" epistemology even before some theorists began revising feminism into a form of post-modernism.

The world-story we have rejected is written in a code whose syntax respects enumerative, statistical and metaphysical generalization. Of these, enumerative generalization is probably kindest to particulars. But it is so weak that to be true such a generalization must do a kind of violence by remarking the unremarkable and unsaying everything that is worth saying about the individuals in question. (For example, I hardly honor my colleagues in the MSU Philosophy Department by saying that they all have offices on the MSU campus, which is the most substantial thing I can think of that I know is really unqualifiedly true of each and every one of them.) Statistical generalization may be the next kindest to particulars since it is cheerful about coexisting with, that is, ignoring, discrepant data. Metaphysical generalization, declaring this or that to be the what-it-is of a thing, threatens the annihilation of that which does not fit its prescription. For example: Women are nurturant; if you are not nurturant you are not a real woman, but a monster. All generalization seems unjust to particulars, as is reflected in the aversion people so commonly have to "being labelled." Generalization subsumes particulars, reduces them to a common denominator. Nomination is domination, or so it seems.

It might seem that in response to the embarrassment of these paradoxes, we should retreat into autobiography or string suitable adjectives onto the noun 'woman', and many of us have tried both. [Speaking as an able-bodied college-educated christian-raised middle-class middle-aged and middle-sized white anglo lesbian living in the midwest, I can report that these strategies both reduce one to silliness and generate serious questions about adjective order in English.] More moderately, we might back up to narrowing the subject of our claims to specific groups of women identified by race, class, nationality or so forth. In some cases we have done this (at the risk, even so, of overgeneralizing or stereotyping), but what we have to say, or what we thought we had to say, is not just a compendium of claims about the circumstances and experiences of women of particular groups. Our project is theoretical, philosophical, political. You have to have some sort of genuinely general generality to have theory, philosophy, politics.

But from the start, feminism has been going at generality in another way. We need to pay more attention to what we have been doing. In consciousness-raising, there is a movement away from the isolation of the individual, the particular. But even in the most culturally homogeneous local consciousness-raising group, women's lives were not revealed to be as alike as two copies of the morning paper; we agreed neither in the details of our experience nor in opinions and judgments. We perceived similarities in our experiences, but we did not determine the relative statistical frequencies of the events and circumstances we found to be "common." And the question of what a woman is, far from being answered, was becoming unanswerable and perhaps unaskable. The generalizing movement of our "science" was not to metaphysical, statistical or universal generalization. In consciousness-raising women engage in a communication that has aptly been called "hearing each other into speech."[7] It is speaking unspoken facts and feelings, unburying the data of our lives. But as the naming occurs, each woman's speech creating context for the other's, the data of our experience reveal patterns both within the experience of one woman and among the experiences of several women. The experiences of each woman and of the women collectively generate a new web of meaning. Our process has been one of discovering, recognizing, and creating patterns—patterns within which experience made a new kind of sense, or in many instances, for the first time made any sense at all. Instead of bringing a phase of enquiry to closure by summing up what is known, as other ways of generalizing do, pattern recognition/construction opens fields of meaning and generates new interpretive possibilities. Instead of drawing conclusions from observations, it generates observations.

Naming patterns is not reductive or totalitarian. For instance, we realize that men interrupt women more than women interrupt men in conversation: we recognize a pattern of dominance in conversation—male dominance. We do not say that every man in every conversation with any woman always interrupts. (We do not hazard a guess, either, as to the exact statistical frequency of this phenomenon, though once someone did a study on it, it turned out to be even higher than any of us suspected.) We do not close any questions about men's awareness of what they are doing, or women's experience of it. What we do is sketch a schema within which certain meanings are sustained. It makes sense of a woman feeling stifled, frustrated, angry or stupid when she is in the company of men. It makes sense of the women who lower the pitch of their voices and used the most elite vocabulary they can command when they want to be heard in a male realm. And when a man repeatedly interrupts me, I do not just dumbly suffer the battery; in knowledge of the pattern, I interpret this event, I know it as an *act*, as "dominating." Recognizing a pattern like this can also lead out along various associative axes to other discoveries. The pattern of conversational interruption readily suggests itself as a simile for the naming of other abridgements, interferences and amputations we suffer but have not named.

Patterns sketched in broad strokes make sense of our experiences, but not a single unified or uniform sense. They make our different experiences intelligible in different ways. Naming patterns is like charting the prevailing winds over a continent; there is no implication that every individual and item in the landscape is identically affected.[8] For instance, male violence patterns experiences as different as that of overprotective paternalism and of incest, as different as the veil and the bikini. The differences of experience and history are in fact necessary to perception of the patterns. It is precisely in the homogeneity of isolation that one *cannot* see patterns and one remains unintelligible to oneself. What we discover when we break into connection with other women cannot possibly be uniform women's experience and perception, or we would discover nothing. It is precisely the articulation and differentiation of the experiences formulated in consciousness-raising that gives rise to meaning. Pattern discovery and invention requires encounters with difference, with variety. The generality of pattern is not a generality that defeats or is defeated by variety.

Our game is pattern perception; our epistemological issues have to do with the strategies of discovering patterns and articulating them effectively, judging the strength and scope of patterns, properly locating the particulars of experience with reference to patterns, understanding the variance of experience from what we take to be a pattern. As I see it the full reflective philosophical discussion of these issues has barely begun, and I cannot write the treatise which develops them either alone or yet. But I will survey some of the territory.

We have used a variety of strategies for discovering patterns, for making sense of what does not make sense. The main thing is to notice what doesn't make sense. Discovering patterns requires novel acts of attention. Consciousness-raising techniques typically promote just such unruliness by breaking the accustomed structures of conversation. Adopting practices designed to give every woman equal voice and equal audience, and to postpone judgment, defense, advocacy and persuasion, the members of the group block the accustomed paths of thought and perception. In the consequent chaos, they slide, wander or break into uncharted semantic space. In this wilderness one can see what doesn't make sense—incongruities, bizarreness, anomaly, unspeakable acts, unthinkable accusations, "semantic black holes."[9] These things are denied, veiled, disguised or hidden by practices and language which embody and protect privileged perceptions and opinions. But they are often, perhaps characteristically, flagged by "outlaw emotions,"[10] and a powerful strategy of discovery therefore is to legitimize an outlaw emotion. You feel something—anger, pain, despair, joy, an erotic rush—which is not what you are supposed to be feeling. Everything invites you to stifle it, decide you are imagining it or are overreacting, or declare yourself crazy or bad. The strategy of discovery, enabled by the consciousness-raising structures, is to put that feeling at the center, let it be presumed normal, appropriate, true, real, and then see how everything else falls out around it. Over and over, for instance, women's pain, once taken simply as pain—real and appropriate pain—discovers and confirms the pattern and reiterated patterns of male violence. Similarly, giving any "minority" voice centrality in the force-field of meanings discovers patterns to us.[11]

Other strategies of pattern perception are all the familiar strategies of creativity and of self-defense: cultivating the ability to be astounded by ordinary things, the capacity for loving attention, confidence in one's senses, a sensitivity to smokescreens and fishy stories, and so on.

Pattern perception and processes of checking such perception also requires recognition that not everything that is intelligibly located by a pattern *fits* the pattern. A great deal of what I have said over the years about women is not true of me (as critics both hostile and friendly have often pointed out) and much of it is not true of most of the women I have said it to. One reason this is so is that many of the patterns we discover are not so much *descriptive* and *prescriptive*—patterns of expectation, bribe and penalty which many individual women manage to deviate from to a greater or lesser extent by rejection, resistance or avoidance. A very significant aspect of feminist theory is an *affirmation* of the disparity between the lived reality of women and the patterns of patriarchy. In the project of making oneself intelligible, it is as useful to recognize forces to which one is *not* yielding as to recognize forces by which one is being shaped or immobilized. For instance, there are kinds of prudishness, "modesty," and shame which shape women's experience of sexuality (not of course in all cultures, but certainly not only in "western" cultures). For the women who are not contaminated by these diseases, it is nonetheless relevant to some of the meanings of their sexual experience that many women are thus shaped, that many men expect women to be so, and that the woman who is exceptional in this respect has acquired her own shape partly in resistance to the force of that mold and/or partly by some form of insulation or obliviousness which surely has other interesting manifestations too. Recognizing the pattern and "placing" herself in the range of meanings it sets up will contribute to her understanding of herself and her world even if she is not a woman restrained and distorted by sexual shame.

But in addition to the fact that individual divergence from the pattern we perceive is not generally to be understood as a disconfirmation of the alleged existence or strength of the pattern, there are limits to how much any one pattern patterns.

Patterns are like metaphors. (Perhaps patterns *are* metaphors.) Just as an illuminating metaphor eventually breaks down when persistently pressed, the patterns that make experience intelligible only make so much of it intelligible at a time, and over time that range may change. In the case of pressing a good metaphor, one finds out a great deal by exploring its limits, understanding where and why it breaks down. Similarly with patterns. An important part of pattern perception is exploring the range of the pattern, and a way of going wrong is misjudging scope.

An example of this sort of mistake that comes from the heart of some important feminist theorizing is in perceptions of patterns of dependence of women on men. Anyone who is oppressing another is very likely exploiting social structures which coerce the other into some kind and degree of dependence upon the oppressor (for otherwise, the victim could and would extricate herself from the situation). But the middle white American pattern of coerced one-on-one economic and psychological dependence of females on males with limited but real opportunities for individual women's *ad hoc* escape from the trap is only a local working out of a higher-order pattern. In many cultural locales dependency is more collective, and/or not primarily economic, is more or less escapable, or more or less extreme. We can err by taking one local expression of the pattern as itself a global pattern, or by thinking there is no such global pattern because we see that not everyone experiences the particular expression of it that has so far been brought to our attention (e.g., assuming that since single women are not economically dependent on a husband, they are independent of men).

If the occupational hazard of pattern perceivers is misjudging scope, the remedy is communication. The strategy by which one proceeds to test pattern recognition involves many inquirers articulating patterns they perceive and running them by as great a variety of others as possible. The others will respond by saying something like "yes, that makes sense, it illuminates my experience" or "that doesn't sound like my life, you're not talking about me." Patterns emerge in the responses and signal the limits of the meaning-making powers of the patterns one has articulated. A pattern is not bogus or fictitious either simply because things don't fit it (for the non-fit may be as powerfully significant as a fit would be) or simply because there are limits to what it patterns.

One might consider requiring of the articulation of patterns that they explicitly signal the limits of their powers and applications, and then criticize those which do not or which signal it wrongly. But the similarity of patterns and metaphors is salient again here. When one says that life is a stage, one does not and cannot specify in precisely what dimensions and to exactly what degree life is stage-like. One aspect of the power of metaphor is the openness of its invitation to interpretation—it casts light of a certain color, but does not determine how its object looks in that light to any particular observer. The patterns articulated by the feminist theorist similarly have the power to make lives and experience usefully intelligible in part because they do *not* fix their own applications, but provide a frame only, for the making of meaning. Neither patterns nor metaphors contain specifications of their limits. They work until they don't work. You find out where that is by working them until they dissolve. Like a metaphor, a pattern has to be appreciated, put to use. You have to run with it. You may outrun its power without realizing you have if you are not paying attention to the voices and perception of many women.

The business of telling when one is just wrong about a pattern, when one is misperceiving, is very tricky for women in our current states of community, or lack of it. We work in a climate of inquiry where a mainstream knowledge industry works constantly to undermine our confidence in our perceptions, where political exigencies tempt us to forced unity, and where everything would keep women from forming epistemic community. In such conditions we operate without clear and dependable intuitions of plausibility and without adequate benefit of the monitoring function provided by a clear sense of audience. It is very hard to know when we are getting it right and when we are off the wall. Our first urgency therefore, built into our situation and our method, is to be engaged with the greatest possible range of perceivers, of theorizers. What we are about is re-metaphoring the world. We need as many and various perceivers as possible to mix metaphors wildly enough so we will never be short of them, never have to push one beyond its limits, just for lack of another to take up where it left off.

The whole female population of the planet is neither a speaker nor an audience. It does not have a story. But communications among women—kin, friends, co-workers, writers and their readers, explorers and the audiences of their stories—have generated world-stories in which the lives and fates of humans on this planet fall out along fault-lines of female and male as prominently and consistently as on faultlines of wealth and of tribal, racial or national identities, and those lines are characterized by women doing more work and controlling less wealth than men, by men doing far more violence to women than women do to men, and by men's world-stories marginalizing, reducing and erasing women. We have not assumed but discovered these patterns and their many ramifications. In this discovery, we have discovered the grounds of epistemic community. It is not a homogeneous community; it does not have to be so in order to ground and validate feminist theory, in fact it *cannot* be so if it is to support the meaning-making of feminist theory.

If a common (but not homogeneous) oppression is what

constitutes us an epistemic community, what will happen when we free ourselves? First, I would suppose that a common history of oppression and liberation would hold us for a long time in a degree of community, but then, eventually, perhaps we will fall into a happy and harmless theoretical disarray. What we are writing, *The World, According to Women,* has never been anything but an anthology, a collection of tales unified, like any yarn, only by successively overlapping threads held together by friction, not riveted by logic. There is no reason to predict or require that it must forever hold together at all. Perhaps eventually the category *woman* will be obsolete. But perhaps not.

(The following is a revision of material that constituted the final section of this essay when I was giving it as talks prior to its publication.)

If the world-writing project of feminist theory does not collapse under the enormous variety of women's experience and perceptions, but in fact requires differences and variety for its process, why do the differences among us give us such trouble? One reason is that some feminist theorists have ourselves sometimes not recognized or understood our own process, which I think is understandable in terms of our own educations and histories, as I explained in the first parts of this paper. Another set of reasons have to do with the race, class and ethnic locations of the theorists. Most of the feminist theorists who are best positioned politically and economically to have the widest audience have been members of groups which are generally privileged in western cultures. The ways our own racism, class bias, and investment in our privileges distort our perceptions have generated both misperception of patterns and unconstructive responses to the corrective influences of other women's perceptions. Beyond that, finally, is a matter of *voice.*

The difference between a totalizing, reducing, dominating generalization and an open friendly pattern perception is not in the words used to put them forth. It is in where they came from and what they are for. And this is expressed and communicated by the *voice* in which the words are uttered.

The voice of the men's world-story is the voice of the speaker who does not have to fit his words to the truth, because the truth will fit his words. Things are true because he says them, he does not say them because they are true. The voice of the men's world-story is the voice whose naming makes things so.[12] If, as Joyce Trebilcot has said, the truth is "what you've gotta believe,"[13] then this is the voice of the one who is authorized to stipulate what you've gotta believe. Words spoken in this voice are really not "about" anything but the will and power of the speaker, and thus anything said in this voice offends everyone and everything it is ostensibly about: to the extent that the words seem to fit those persons or things it is only because the words are just reinforcing the will and power that have already molded the persons and things to fit the words. People who have learned to recognize the sound of this voice but are not themselves authorized to *use* it, cannot tolerate its pronouncements about them; *everything* it says is damaging, reducing, annihilating. Think of women listening to Freud's theories about women, or of African-Americans reading the sober social scientific theories about the demise of the Black family; think of how well-meaning white-Anglo accounts of alcoholism among Native Americans sound to those who are Native Americans.[14]

Now consider the highly educated white feminist theorist standing in her relatively privileged position for speaking and being heard. She has rightly enough assumed the moral high ground in a certain domain of concern; she is rightly delighted and justly empowered by her recent discovery of the authority of her own experience and perception; she is rightly confident of the importance of what she has to say. She knows it is right and proper (epistemologically, politically, morally) for her to be a full participant in world-construction. In what voice will she speak, now that she has assumed the authority to speak? Given the pervasive *de facto* race and class segregation in which she has lived, and given the education she has had, there is only one voice she has ever heard that is a voice with authority: the voice of the white male speaking *ex cathedra*. A likely disaster is that she will not speak in a new voice of her own but in her father's voice. And if she does it is likely that many women in her audience (especially those who cannot imagine *themselves* speaking in that voice) will hear only what is damaging, reducing, annihilating.

This matter of voice seems to me not to be a superficial thing. It is more fundamental, I think, than something like using a specialist's jargon to make a point that could have been made in a common vocabulary. A patient listener can, perhaps with some help, translate the jargon and find out that something useful has been said; but this voice is one in which nothing useful can be said (useful, that is, to any purpose but that of oppression), even when its utterances apparently "fit the facts." This *is* the voice whose nomination is domination. It is the voice that accompanies and reinforces the arrogant eye.[15] It is not possible to articulate friendly, cooperative, reciprocally empowering perceptions of patterns in this voice.

The voices of patriarchal authority drone in unhearing unison. For some feminists, one of the things on the agenda of feminist praxis might be re-training their/our voices (and ears) to registers that harmonize and are attuned to harmonies.

I cannot say just how this might be done, of course, but some ideas about it do come to mind. Voice is not vocabulary, but it is associated with vocabulary, and acquiring voices of our own may be considerably aided by original lexical playfulness and by refraining from rushing to adopt each new linguistic fashion of the Euro-American intelligentia. Also (a not unrelated point), what voices one can project is surely related to what voices one hears and responds to. We might acquire friendlier voices by listening in friendly and responsive ways to the voices of more other women—a listening that I have already suggested is central to the success of the collective project of pattern perception and meaning-making.

If some of us are speaking in the wrong voice, that suggests we are hearing the wrong voices or hearing in some wrong way, and that our theorizing will also be "off." And if this is so, then clearly the matter of voice is integral to the project of pattern perception and meaning-making; there is no separation of what is expressed and the mode of expression. For many women, if not for all, re-training voices will be integral to re-telling the world.

    [1] This essay was published in *Theoretical Perspectives on Sexual Difference*, edited by Deborah L. Rhode (New Haven, Conn.: Yale University Press, 1990). An earlier version of it was delivered as an invited paper on the program of the Central Division of the American Philosophical Association, May 1, 1987, and the earliest work on it was supported by the Center For The Study of Women in Society at the University of Oregon where I was a visiting scholar in 1984-85. I am indebted at many points to conversations with

Carolyn Shafer, and to comments made by many women on the various occasions over the last five years when I have given talks in which I was working out various aspects of these thoughts.

[2] Deborah Rhode suggested that what I am saying here is simply that women's experience appears to be "different." But in the current lingo, influenced by the French, "difference" is an abstract and generic term. What I am referring to here is two quite specific things—that which is flat out unintelligible (which is not quite what the French, following Derrida and in the shadow of Lacan, meant by "difference"), and that which is specifically and concretely "different" in that it is abnormal, in the negatively charged sense of that concept. I am talking here from the experience of women. We do not experience ourselves, under the conceptual net of patriarchal forms, as abstractly and semantically "different," but as unintelligible or abnormal. So, also, do men commonly experience women.

[3] The use here of "we," "our," "feminist theorists" and "feminist theory" is and will remain problematic. I know I am not the only one engaged in the pilgrimage described here, but I could not and would not pretend to say who else this speaks for. For those who do not identify with this "we," I think the essay can be read as a record of what *some* women who have called themselves feminists and theorists have thought and done.

[4] This approach is perhaps the general tendency of which the "feminist empiricism" described by Sandra Harding is a more specific instance. See Harding, *The Science Question in Feminism* (Ithaca, N.Y.: Cornell University Press, 1986) pp. 24-5, passim.

[5] This dogma has been questioned within that same tradition, but it still has power in contemporary thinking. The "post-modern" critique of this tradition's concepts of truth, reality and knowledge is by no means universally acknowledged as sound, and furthermore the transformation of worldview that would be involved in actually abandoning those concepts is more profound than most of us can manage in less than a decade or so.

[6] Cf., Maria Lugones, "Playfulness, 'World'-Travelling, and Loving Perception," *HYPATIA: A Journal of Feminist Philosophy*, Volume II, Number 2, Spring, 1987.

[7] This phrase was coined by Nelle Morton, in a talk given at an American Academy of Religion Workshop, December 28, 1977 (cited in Mary Daly, *Gyn/Ecology* [Boston: Beacon Press, 1978], p.313).

[8] For some elaboration on this point see the introduction to my book *The Politics of Reality: Essays in Feminist Theory* (Trumansburg, NY: The Crossing Press, 1983) pp. xii-xiv.

[9] This term due to Ruth Ginzberg, in conversation.

[10] This phrase, as used in this context, is due to Alison Jaggar.

[11] The centering of a Black woman's voice and views as accomplished in bell hooks' *Feminist Theory: From Margin to Center* (Boston: South End Press, 1984) is a good example of this. The entire phenomenon of U.S. feminism looks very different when cast as relatively marginal to a center in the lives and interests of Black and poor women, than when cast as central to History.

[12] In my essay, "Some Reflections on Separatism and Power," in *The Politics of Reality* (Freedom, Cal.: The Crossing Press, 1983), pp. 105-106, I discuss the use of the power of naming things.

[13] That is how Joyce Trebilcot put the point in a discussion. In print she said, "In dominant culture 'truths' are presented as claims that people are required to accept as bases for their thinking and action and hence identities, regardless of how *they* feel about the 'truths' and regardless of their relevant experiences. . . . [M]en are able not only to project their personalities as reality, but also to require that other people participate in those realities and accept them as their own. Recipients of the 'truth' (ie., all those not certified to create it) are expected to long for truth, to respect it, to bow down to it, and especially, to honor—and obey—those who are authorities on it." "Dyke Methods," in *Lesbian Philosophies and Cultures*, edited by Jeffner Allen (Albany, NY: State University of New York Press, 1990), pp. 16-17.

[14] Note the connection here with the passage in my essay, "On Being White" (*The Politics of Reality* (Freedom, Cal.: The Crossing Press, 1983), pp. 112-113) about the woman whose father can say nothing that is not damaging.

[15] See "In and Out of Harm's Way," in *The Politics of Reality*, by Marilyn Frye (Freedom, Cal.: The Crossing Press, 1983).

Four
Reviews

The Contest of Feminisms[1]

A review of *Feminist Politics and Human Nature*, by Alison Jaggar
(Totowa, New Jersey: Rowman & Allanheld, 1983.)

This is an ambitious and very interesting book. Jaggar undertakes to identify, compare and criticize the major schools of
contemporary feminist thought, and to show which is the best of
the lot and why. As scholarship, it covers an enormous amount
of ground; as politics, it is bold; in its central and most conten-
tious argument, it is challenging.

The book begins with the claim that all political philosophies presuppose theories of human nature and any complete and distinctive political philosophy is grounded in a coherent and distinctive theory of human nature. (By a "theory of
human nature" she means interdependent conceptions of what it
is to be a human being and what constitutes such a being's well-
being.) She argues that feminism is political philosophy and thus
it is possible and illuminating to distinguish feminism from non-
feminism, and to identify and compare the various feminisms, in
terms of underlying theories of human nature. And this she
undertakes to do, comparing and contrasting Marxist, liberal,
radical and socialist feminisms—discussing each in a chapter on
its theory of human nature and a chapter on its politics.

The first sign that the project is not as neatly conceived
as it may sound is in Jaggar's justifications of her selection of
certain feminisms and not others for inclusion in it. She claims to
identify political theories (feminisms) by reference to their distinctive theories of human nature and she justifies treating neither Black feminism nor anarchist feminism as discrete feminist
theories by saying in each case that it is not identifiable in terms
of a single distinctive conception of human nature. But she goes

on to identify radical feminism as a discrete political theory in spite of her claim that it does not have a single conception of human nature, and she excludes from the project both existentialist and "religious" feminisms even though they are, among feminisms, probably the most consciously grounded in the most articulate theories of human nature. The groundedness of political theories in theories of human nature does not after all play quite the central organizing role here that Jaggar claims for it.

As the plot unfolds, it turns out (*contra* her claim on page 10) that Jaggar is not laying out four distinct political theories with four distinctive theories of human nature, but three theories and something which by her lights is not a political theory (radical feminism) which are variously related to two theories of human nature—the Marxist and the liberal. The theories of human nature which, according to Jaggar, underlie all of the four feminisms are presented as more or less closely approximating or deviating from these two.

As Jaggar sees it, the liberal sort of view of human nature is wrong because it is static, ahistorical and essentialist: being human consists in being rational, which is a timeless and unchanging property inherent in whatever individuals have it. The Marxist sort of view is right because it is dynamic, historical materialist and dialectical: being human is being an animal whose ever-changing nature is determined dialectically in *praxis*. Jaggar's analyses suggest that all feminisms tend to evolve toward a Marxist sort of view of human nature simply because the more one understands the structures of sexism and the oppression of women the more obvious it becomes that they cannot be criticized or resisted in any way that would bring a fundamental change (women's liberation) so long as one accepts the static and androcentric concepts of *woman*, *man*, and *human* that they presuppose. Even Marxist feminism, developing toward Jaggar's socialist feminism, has to become in a sense more Marxist by taking the categories *woman* and *man* as no more "given" or "natural" than the category *human*.

The chapters on radical feminism and socialist feminism are the heart of the book. Jaggar fully recognizes the creative and profound contributions of radical feminism to our understanding of the oppression of women, but she rejects radical feminism and argues the superiority of socialist feminism. After I emerged from grappling with the details of the arguments, my post-struggle feeling was that there is really not much difference between the two. It seems that most feminists in both groups would generally agree in respect to the following fundamental propositions or attitudes:

- the oppression of women is not an epiphenomenon of any other dominance-subordinance system such as capitalism or racism;
- sex, sexuality and reproduction are "political" and the traditional private/public distinction is untenable;
- women are a political class which cuts across boundaries of economic class, race and nationality;
- compulsory heterosexuality and motherhood for women is a central phenomenon of the subordination of women to men;
- the processes of political action and change are as important as their products;
- capitalism is inconsistent with the liberation of women.

And this is by no means a complete list of what might be "points of unity" for both radical and socialist feminists.

What Jaggar accepts of radical feminism (and she accepts it pretty warmly and with few reservations) is its description of the world as perceived in the experience of women—the feminist description of male-dominated social order. (She of course notes its incompleteness due to lack of expression of the experience of women of all races, classes and so on.) What she faults radical feminism for is what she sees as its failure to construct a political theory grounded in an adequate concept of human nature, and its consequent failure (as she sees it) to provide the necessary foundation for a political movement which can succeed. She argues that socialist feminism can provide such a foundation.

For political action to succeed, according to Jaggar, it must be determined by a strategy which is suggested by an account of the causes of the social conditions which one wants to change. A description of the social phenomenon in question is not a causal explanation of it and is therefore not sufficient to generate effective strategies for change; an adequate political theory does provide the needed causal explanation. Jaggar says that radical feminists have generated radically new, compelling and vivid descriptions of men and their behavior and the female-subordinating institutions of patriarchal cultures (at least Euro-American cultures) but have not provided answers to *why* men are like that, *why they behave like that*, why the institutions are what they are; and thus no coherent strategy for change is generated. She thinks that one reason radical feminists have failed in this way is that they tend to take an ahistorical view of society and human beings, due to having one of their own historical feet in liberal civil rights politics and philosophy; one does not give causal explanations of things perceived as having no history.

On page 289, Jaggar says radical feminism "does not explain the material reasons for men's subjugation of women." My own marginal note there says: "men do it to gain material services and psychological benefits attainable by that means." This seems to me to be a radical feminist's answer, and to be "material" enough and "causal" enough to suggest strategies for change. But Jaggar pushes the question back. Why do men go after these benefits this way? Is it because anyone with the opportunity would thus exploit others (humans are evil), or because *males* are like that (males are evil)? She seems to think that radical feminists are stuck with picking one of these two "biologistic" answers, and socialist feminists are not. It is perfectly true that some of the writers one would likely classify as radical feminists do give the second of these answers (and only a certain ontological faith "proves" they are wrong), but I do not see anything in the general drift of radical feminist thought which compels it. Many of us would say "none of the above" and go on to say any human being whose nature was the nature of a man as constructed in male-dominated societies would be like that, given the opportunity, and would also as a matter of "business as usual" do the sorts of things which continuously recreate the opportunity. We can locate the cause (but not The Ultimate Cause) in men's natures and yet not in *men's nature* conceived as genetically given. (And we might locate some more causes in the natures of women as constructed in male-dominated societies.) We could go on, as many of us have, to locate the causes of these natures in both material and ideological structures in such societies and to try to devise strategies for evolving different structures.

With Jaggar's criticism of radical feminism in mind as I read the chapter on socialist feminist, I was looking for her account of the cause of men's ways of being and behaving, and of woman-subordinating institutions existing and being as they are. But no such account is there. She changes the subject, "historicizing" it, and addresses the question of the causes of the particular form the subordination of women takes at this historical time and place, that is, in contemporary capitalist societies. She then says that it takes the form it takes ("alienation") because of the fetishism of commodities, the rise of positive science, the separation of home from workplace, the split between emotion and reason, the distinction between the personal and the political and so on (p.317). That is, the reason the subjugation of women takes the form it takes in capitalistic societies in the modern era is that they are modern and capitalistic.

By analogy, one can distinguish between the question of why humans adorn themselves and why human adornment takes the form it does in Euro-American cultures in the latter part of the twentieth century. The latter can be partially answered in terms of the structures of the prevailing form of capitalism. But that leaves the former unanswered. Women are subordinated to men in many, if not all, societies known to euro-american literati. Explanations of the forms this takes in the different societies are not explanations of this global phenomenon. My guess is that there is no such thing as giving a causal explanation of why humans adorn themselves, and also no such thing as giving a causal explanation of why women are subordinated to men (with local variations of cultural form and detail). I think that Jaggar might agree with me in the view that the only things we can causally explain are more local perturbations in the river of human existence. But then radical feminists are not to be faulted for failing to explain "the subordination of women by men," and radical feminists have been as ready to give local causal explanations as Jaggar is. The explanations suggested by radical feminists only give material relations of production less centrality and emphasize more the mechanisms of the reproduction of culture.

I think that socialist feminists and radical feminists not only share many fundamental beliefs but also at the theoretical bottom are up against the same perplexing mysteries.

Jaggar's explanation of "the material reasons for men's subjugation of women" has to do with features of capitalism. But if capitalism determines that some group has to be in charge of compulsive commodity consumption, occupy the "private" realm, be the repository of "emotion," etc., what determines that that group should be women, females? Why shouldn't it be the males? Or the fat or the thin, or the redheads, or both females and males of certain non-noble lineages? That such a functional cut is made at all might be explicable in terms of capital; that it is made along the line of genital sex and that the females rather than the males are put on the down side is not explained by capital but by sexism. And a socialist feminist is right back with the rest of the feminists in explaining *that*. Why is there sexism? Why are the lines drawn by sex, and why are women on the down side? I do not see how socialist feminism can rescue us from having to wonder if this is finally going to have to be explained in terms of biological reproductive functions, or not explained at all. And if it comes to that, I would opt for no explanation at all, since I don't think we need one in order to have plausible strategies for change. And this may be the only major point on which I would disagree with Jaggar.

[1] First published in *The Center Review*, The Center for the Study of Women in Society, University of Oregon, May, 1986. I am indebted to all the women who participated in the CSWS ovular in the Spring of 1985, when we discussed this book, though I would not assume any of them agree with what I say in this review.

Feminism and the "New" Physics[1]

A review of *The Anatomy of Freedom: Feminism, Physics and Global Politics*, by Robin Morgan (Garden City, NY: Anchor Press/ Doubleday, 1982)

Like most of Robin Morgan's writings, this book is intensely autobiographical and deliberately provocative of personal response. I like the personal, the poetic and the theoretical being intermixed; I like an author's being strongly present in her work. But in this case I think it wise to hold back and refuse her invitation to personal involvement, for the invitation is at best ambivalent. For instance, she introduces a guided tour of her own body images as an engagement so intense and complete that "you might not emerge from here unborn," but only a few sentences later warns the reader off: "...you can neither find nor lose yourself here; I'm much too crowded already." At worst she will make a patsy of you. She covers her gratuitous admission that her husband wrote some passages of the book by claiming everyone else's collaboration too: "You, too, have written certain passages in this book when you thought you were merely playing. Do you know which passages?" This is coercive, cooptive, and condescending. Not to mention cute.

My second reason for resisting the personal engagement Morgan would seduce the reader into is that I think she is importantly and fundamentally wrong in this book, and that should be said from a respectful distance.

Robin Morgan has paid a lot of dues. She had a significant part in the new articulation of feminism that burst upon America[2] in the middle and late 60's; she stumped the states stirring up the new Women's Liberation Movement; she has demonstrated, petitioned, occupied, speechified, written poetry, read poetry, marched and been arrested. Many feminists in these early 80's are indebted to her, often in ways we do not even know—intellectually, artistically, and for wholesome examples of daring and brashness. *The Anatomy of Freedom* is meant to make the same kind of contribution, of leadership and inspiration, to the second generation of this movement.

The book covers a lot of ground. She talks of images of the self—dream selves, body images, old and young selves. She mixes and connects her topics nicely—joining, for example, "the American family," international feminist networking, and American racism in a chapter subtitled "An Anatomy of Kin." The chapter subtitled "An Anatomy of Mortality" is about children and the meaning of old age. Chapter IV, on sexual passion, includes a very interesting discussion of desire as curiosity and "sexual fundamentalism" as the effort, out of fear, to suppress curiosity (and hence, also, intelligence); it also has a section titled "Remedial Living" which is about an affair she had with a virile young man whom she apparently neither respected nor liked very much. There is a long chapter on technology and women's position with respect to it (and/or in fear of it). And the last quarter of the book is explicitly about physics and feminism.

It is the importing of ideas from physics (the so-called "New Physics") that Morgan sees as bringing something fresh and hopeful to her re-vision and re-articulation of feminism.[3] She has been sparked by the metaphors the physicists use, and she exploits the history of physics for examples of radical reconceptualization to which she can point when explaining that feminism generates and requires reconstruction of one's world view. I agree that the conceptual shifts from classical mechanics to quantum physics are useful analogues of the shifts of consciousness feminism involves. Beyond that, her connecting of physics and feminism seems to me both forced and a great mistake.

Morgan's theorizing does not connect firmly, not always intelligibly, with the concepts and theories of physics, or with its uses of its language. For instance, she says: "Let's call our framework the F-matrix Theory, equated as $F=et^2$ or: *Feminism equals equality/empowerment/evolution times the squared velocity of transformation.*" This use of "$F=et^2$" is so remote from any use of equations in physics as to make importing such a pattern of symbols into this context seem to be merely a gimmick. Equations are not slogans, and slogans, which have their own perfectly respectable powers, do not acquire either the prestige or the empirical meaning of scientific generalizations by being expressed in the format of equations. By my reading, there is throughout the book a great deal of this sort of adventitious use of the verbal and conceptual apparatus of physics, while I find the use of it only rarely illuminating.

Morgan trusts physics and physicists. She quotes from the books warmly and with confidence. She begins one section with the incautious phrase, "The New Physics has taught us..." Her physicists are probably right enough about physics (though they will be displaced too, in a while, by a fresh crop of Newer Physicists), but their imaginations and metaphors have been shaped within an intellectual establishment which is one of the most persistently male-dominated and elitist of them all, and they are engaged in popularizing their knowledge and themselves, which is not and could not be a politically innocent undertaking. Listen to them, in their own words and in Morgan's paraphrases of them:

> Mass doesn't exist per se; mass is merely a form of energy.

> ...energy itself (which is all there is)...

> The solid, material body is an illusion...it is all a matter of energy.

> Quantum theory has demolished the classical concepts of solid objects.

> Mass is simply a form of energy.

> The universe begins to look more like a great thought than a great machine.

> Everything is energy.

and in a list of descriptions of beliefs which are said to be obsolete:

> Material and matter are seen as real.

The mathematical relationship of energy and mass could be interpreted to mean that mass and energy are (equally) different modes of being of the same ultimate "stuff." But this rhetoric translates the mathematics into a hierarchical one-way reductive identification: *Matter is really energy.* And the fact that quantum physics does not make use of the concept of matter that is employed in classical mechanics is given over as: *Matter is not real; the solid, material body is an illusion.* Morgan quotes one scientist as saying, "All of astrophysics is about nature's attempt to release the energy in matter." Listen to the language. Nature is featured as an agent with a will and purpose, the purpose being to transform matter into energy—a transformation which leaves *no matter.* Accordingly, the "natural" progress of the universe is toward a world without matter. Matter is conceived as something whose natural destiny is to be annihilated.

In the rhetoric of the "New Physics" matter is something illusory, temporary, static, cosmically primitive; in this New Pythagoreanism, all is energy. Throughout Morgan's book energy is associated with motion, freedom and joy, while matter is associated with stasis, rigidity, confinement and oppression. There is nothing new about this. This is Plato; this is christianity; this is spirit-body dualism; this is misogyny. Matter. Mater. Body. Flesh. Woman. The rhetoric and imagery of the so-called New Physics, as popularized in a recent flood of fashionable books, is the same old stuff passed off as a new and optimistic, playful science. It makes me dizzy to see someone like Robin Morgan thinking it might be a vehicle for a new, optimistic and joyful feminism.

Though she is a poet, no mean scholar of misogyny and a conscious rebel against body-loathing, Morgan apparently did not hear these scary mythic meanings of the rhetoric of the popularized physics. I think this may be because her interest in the physics was not after all primarily a poet's attraction to metaphors; it really is the *physics*, not the language, that she had an important use for. This comes out in the chapter on marriage.

The chapter on marriage is about her own marriage and is as central to this book as Marriage is to Patriarchy. Though she gives reasons for using the word 'marriage', she insists that she is *"not* speaking about *the institution of marriage"* but about "the complex holography involved in any two persons (of any sex) living together as sexual lovers, and in a more or less long-term emotional bond of partnership which can include economic, social, aesthetic, political, etc. sharing of resources." When the "persons of any sex" are in fact a woman and a man who are legally married, this distinction does not hold up, and

Morgan herself points to many of the reasons why it cannot. In her discussion of children and sex, she is very clear on the point that power differences between two people inescapably keep "partnership" from being simple partnership. "When somebody much older, taller, or physically stronger is involved, then it's less a question of sex than of *power*...and when an imbalance of power is going on in a sexual relationship, we ought by now to know how deeply destructive that is." She says her husband is significantly older than she, given what she says about her own stature he is probably taller and physically stronger than she, and as a white male and a legal husband he certain has more social and economic power than she.[4] She also cites articles and quotes which draw attention to the fact that a marriage contract creates a legal relationship frighteningly like that of chattel slavery. In spite of her efforts not to treat this marriage as a Marriage (as in "the institution of marriage") she must know it is one. In fact, this chapter reads as a history of the struggle to make a Marriage into a partnership, and it expresses perhaps more effectively than she would wish a longing, almost a craving, for the reconciliation which has not been achieved. As she says in the first chapter, the struggle is not yet even a struggle for freedom, but still, so far, only for the bare idea of freedom. And it is physics which she thinks can provide an analogy which will make liberation from Marriage, Man and Woman, and the reconciliation of "sexless, ageless, raceless brain[s] and heart[s]" conceivable.

> Quantum physics shattered two basic assumptions of classical science—causality and determinism—and opened up the internal, microcosmic universe. If a higher magnification of the seemingly solid body of the marriage can be managed, then that solid, fixed, intransigent form will disappear via the examination...At a higher magnification still, the particles reveal themselves as reconstitutable wholes, each with its own inviolable integrity—no matter how they have seemed to merge, seemed to affirm or resent the merging.

According to physics, rigidity, stasis, closure, fixedness are all, as a matter of good sound science, *appearances* bound to and dependent upon particular circumstances of observation; nothing, nothing at all, remains constant through variations in circumstances of observation. Riding the analogy: the merger, the

Marriage—the intransigent, fixed, solid structure—is a seeming thing, its immutability an illusion, a mere appearance dependent upon the position and situation of the observer.

We travelled the slogan "The personal is political" out to where we could grasp the bars of our cages, the rigid and unyielding structures of material and ideological force which are the causes that determine so much of what we do and what happens to us. Many women thought those structures could be changed in our time by good will, good sex, good analysis and good organizing. And perhaps our individual and joint efforts have changed them slightly, here and there. But generally they have proven intransigent indeed, and the deep weariness, the frustration, the great hunger of the tired, tired revolutionaries are taking their toll. With a surge of desperate hope, Morgan reverses the slogan to travel back to the "internal microcosmic universe," thinking that a change of focus will prove that the solidity of the bars of this cage, like the solidity of matter, was mere appearance, mere illusion, dependent on the situation of the observer.

It doesn't work. A woman's body and a man's fist are exactly as fragile and as solid as they are. The principles of classical mechanics still describe the behavior of middle-sized objects, even when they are understood as a special subset of the principles of the new physics. And anyway, no matter the progress of physics, a broken nose is a broken nose is a broken nose. The fixedness, durability and rigidity of the institutions which shape and determine the adversarial oppositions of women and men are not illusory. It is not true, what Morgan suggests in the first chapter and tries to believe in the fifth, that unfreedom is an illusion. It cannot be cured by an act of imagination—at least not by this one. The buoyant and buoying optimism of Morgan's belief that she has found a way to reconciliation will be tremendously attractive to many feminist readers, for whom a good dose of optimism is much needed these days. But the energy of the work is in some part due to a discordant tension between Morgan's vision of salvation and her own solid knowledge of the simple, mundane, perversely non-biodegradable reality of the oppression of women by men. The tension is often hard to recognize because she veils, disguises and sometimes disowns that knowledge. The author of this book no longer affirms all her transformations.

It was in her poem "The Network of the Imaginary Mother" that Robin Morgan said, "I disown/none/of my transformations...I affirm/all/of my transformations" (*Lady of the Beasts* [NY: Random House, 1976], pp.63-88). In *The Anatomy of Freedom* she systematically disowns both her former selves and her selves in other women. She mentions her own participation in the radical thinking of the late sixties, most often only to say she has now outgrown and transcended such thought. For example, "There we were, feministically aware of the problem (sexism) and able to exchange grown-up names for how it worked (objectification, socialization, commercialization, internalization, and various other -ations)." In general, she speaks with trivializing condescension of those selves, hers and ours, who really took feminist politics seriously—who took seriously, for instance, the idea that appearance and costume have political meaning and thus cut our hair, stopped shaving our legs, stopped wearing high-heeled shoes. She has special contempt for the selves (including her own) who explored or tried to explore lesbian love when it seemed not so much physically compelling as a logically compelling outcome of honestly and consistently held feminist politics. In this case and in others she trivializes women and women's actions by describing feminists' adventures and experiments as capitulations to political pressure rather than as conscientious (and sometimes very exciting and beneficial) attempts to synthesize political thought and personal action. (And you would never know from Morgan that some of the experiments with lesbian love *were* fueled by lively physical desire.) Her world is littered with women she pointedly disowns, women who have taken one or another feminist idea and, by Morgan's lights, Gone Too Far: "extreme matriarchists," goddess worshippers, biological determinists, "earth Mothers," non-monogamists, women who play the men's games, separatists, "self-styled radical feminists," and so on and on.

Morgan's most hostile disassociation from other women is from women who believe that SM and/or pornography are defensible. Having characterized "sexual fundamentalists" as, among other things, people who see sexual practices other than their own as "sick," Morgan herself characterizes women who defend SM and/or pornography as "damaged," and tells the rest of us we certainly should move "beyond taking them seriously." She is sure "such women can realize that what they, in their piteously twisted sexuality, are upholding has nothing, nothing to do with the feminist vision of freedom." With this decisive amputation Morgan destroys any usefulness her ideas about sexual fundamentalism, sexual energy and sexual violence might have had in the perplexing controversies about SM and pornography.

If any of the apparently immutable structures which trap us are illusory and escapable by acts of imagination, it might be some of those which alienate women from ourselves and each other. But the reconciliation for which Morgan yearns is not that one. It is women's and men's alienation from each other that torments her. *The Anatomy of Freedom* is, profoundly, a book for the consolation of heterosexual feminist people. It is certainly strong enough that many will be invigorated by its enthusiasms, but I cannot see that it could change their lives.

Robin Morgan herself, I think, will not be consoled. The great tension in this book suggests that the rash and willful girlchild at the center of her will finally settle for nothing less than the dance *and* the revolution.[5]

[1] This review was published in *The New Women's Times Feminist Review*, 29, September/October 1983.

[2] [I would not now use the term 'America' when I mean the United States or North America. Such usage seems to me to erase Latin America. 1992]

[3] I don't agree with Morgan that current feminisms are generally so sunk in negativity, obsession and alienation as to need quite the degree of radical refreshment she perceives a need for, but perhaps some of what inspires my confidence inspires her despair.

[4] Though her portrait of her marriage seems very intimate, she does not mention their financial resources or their management of contraception, matters which are usually very much involved in the distributions of power between husbands and wives.

[5] [In an interview in off our backs in 1989 (vol. xix, no.4, April), Robin Morgan says that before her book The Demon Lover (Norton, 1989) "I perhaps was hedging by bets a little bit on the "men, bad—women,good" issue...because there was that self-censoring aspect of the married woman." She talks about changes in her politics that did not come about "until I fell in love with a woman" and "a whole perspective of other kinds of sexuality, an energy of eroticism that was not in some ways self-defeating, became conceivable." She goes on to talk about her marriage, in the past tense, saying there was a "power differential" in it "that was a great grief to both of us because we were conscious." This interview suggests that I was right in thinking that this book's attempt at reconciliation was not working for her and would have to lead to something else. 1992]

Courting Gender Justice[1]

A review of *Sexual Harassment of Working Women* by Catharine A. MacKinnon (Yale University Press, New Haven and London, 1979)

The title of this book is a little misleading. Catharine Mac-Kinnon is a lawyer who sees sexual harassment as central to the oppression of women as practiced in western industrialized countries. Her book is about law and liberation. She focusses on anti-discrimination law and the liberation of the workplace, but she sees a woman's work as integral to her social status and sees sexual harassment as expressive of "the pervasive reality of normal relations between the sexes (p.220)."

> Sexual harassment at work connects the jobs most women do...with the structure of sexual relations...with the denigrated economic status women as a gender occupy throughout the society (p.220).

She discusses the application of anti-discrimination laws in cases of sexual harassment in the workplace, but she also sees anti-discrimination law as potentially a very strong force for the dismantling of the structures of oppression generally.

MacKinnon argues that of the parts of the law that seem as though they might offer hope for legal redress for sexual harassment—criminal law, tort law and anti-discrimination law—the latter is the most promising. Even the latter, however, is not too promising on the approach or interpretation of it that has been dominant in the courts. She distinguishes between a "differences" approach and an "inequality" approach, and argues that only when it is approached in the latter way is anti- discrimination law likely to be useful to victims of sexual harassment. The parts of the book (Chapters 5 and 6) which elaborate this distinction between the two approaches are certainly the most difficult parts. I found the argument in these sections not always clean, clear and well-focussed. She comes at the distinction from many different angles and shows its ramifications in many different situations; eventually the different explanations become entangled with each other and some clarity is lost. The distinction, though, is vital both to understanding the ins and outs of anti-discrimination law and to clarity in our conception of equality and of race and gender justice.

The "differences" approach rests on a picture which is rooted in what I think of as a relatively primitive political vision (one which was mine, when I first started trying to say what sexism is). That picture might typically arise out of the experience of seeing females and males treated differently where there seems to be nothing in the real differences between them that would justify the difference of treatment. One notices, for instance, the tracking of boys into Shop and girls into Home Ec. One can see nothing about boys or girls considered in themselves which seems to have anything at all to do with whatever differences there are between wrenches and egg beaters. The tracking seems arbitrary. And since advantage and disadvantage turns on it, it seems unjust. Making arbitrary distinctions in the distribution of advantages and disadvantages is unjust, is sexist or racist, is discrimination. And that is what, on this picture, the law should forbid. One important consequence of this view is that it is not unjust to distribute advantages and disadvantages according to distinctions which are supported by real differences. So, if girls really do mature faster than boys, it would not be unjust to provide girls with certain physical challenges at a younger age than to boys, and hence to give girls a head-start in the "race" for certain benefits.

This Differences Doctrine (which I would call the "arbitrariness" approach) presupposes that there are determinate "real" differences between females and males and that one knows what they are. As a matter of fact there is neither any general agreement on what they are nor agreement on how one could find out what they are. The courts, working within this framework have, of course, gone ahead and decided what are the real differences in various cases.

This reliance upon notions of real differences raises another sort of problem too. By the time female and male humans have been processed and packaged by a sexist culture, the human traits and syndromes do indeed fall out into different constellations which are more or less characteristic of women and of men (given some variations with race and class and so on). These add up to differences between women and men which may have little or no rational relation to anything innate in either sort of beast. We could take these as real differences or see them as "artificial" or "socially constructed." If we let them count as real differences they can be used in justifications of differential distributions of advantages and disadvantages. (Women are more patient with picky repetitive tasks so women should do picky repetititive tasks.) If we don't allow these differences to be used this way, if we don't let them count as "real" for these purposes, then they also cannot be cited in justifications for making discriminations which would help revise or make up for these differences (e.g., state funding for self-defense training for women).

This bind reminds me of Pat Parker's poem, where she says to white women that they should just forget that she's Black...and not ever forget it. Is the white woman supposed to act color-blind, or notice that Black women are Black? Is the law supposed to be gender-blind, or notice that women are Women? The answer requires a shift from a focus on differences and distinctions to a focus on consequences. One's acts and practices should be such as to repair damage done and prevent more damage being done. Sometimes that requires making an advantaging distinction on the basis of a difference, sometimes it requires identical treatment of two people or groups in spite of their difference, sometimes it requires some sort of treatment which reverses or mirror-images a difference. What matters is the outcome, in individual benefit, in benefits to a disadvantaged class, in restructuring a situation in order to prevent continuance of disadvantage. And this is the approach of the other legal doctrine MacKinnon describes—the Inequality Doctrine. It is an approach which begins by taking into account the social reality of hierarchy, differential social status of groups, differential power and unequal distribution of benefits, and aims to create a situation of equality through legally mandating action and practice which will tend to correct damage already done and legally forbidding action and practice which tend to perpetuate the structures which do the damage. This approach does not presuppose a set of real differences and demand that distinctions be based on them; it presupposes that for practical purposes we should assume all differences are socially constructed (or almost all) and that they should be built upon, altered or ignored, depending on what will effect equalization of benefits, opportunities, advantages, and social and economic status.

Part of Mackinnon's purpose in this book is to articulate and promote the "inequality" approach to anti-discrimination law, and to argue that the best hope for litigation of sexual harassment cases lies in anti-discrimination law thus interpreted. Anyone who is considering taking legal action in a case of sexual harassment should read this book and require her lawyer to read it. It will provide invaluable clues about how to present the case so that the presentation steers the court toward an "inequality" interpretation of the anti-discrimination laws and educates the court in the economic, moral and political subtleties of sexual harassment.

While MacKinnon gives good reasons to litigate under the anti-discrimination laws if you are going to go to court, she does not convince me to go to court. She does not (and does not intend to) paint a rosy picture of what the law is currently doing for (to) women. Much of the book is given to exposing in analytic detail the follies of prosecutors, judges and juries as they stumble, not always innocently, among confusions about coercion, false identification of the sexual and the personal, false polarization of the normal and the criminal, confusion of desire and contempt and silly notions of resistance and consent. The heart of the book is devoted largely to showing the perverseness of anti-discrimination law as it has most often been actually applied in cases having to do with discrimination against women.

In spite of all this, MacKinnon has a very optimistic vision of what anti-discrimination law could be. She says that the approach she promotes would be "a substantive approach to discrimination that would overturn the systematic subordination of women (p.117)." She says this doctrine of discrimination "reaches for a political strategy to guide legal intervention on behalf of the less powerful against those who are not likely to relinquish their place (p.127)." This is a legal doctrine according to which "the prohibition on sex discrimination aims to eliminate the social inferiority of one sex to the other, to dismantle the social structure that maintains a series of

practices that cumulatively...'disadvantages' women (p.103)."
It is a doctrine according to which the purpose of the policy
against sex discrimination is "to eliminate the legal supports
for male supremacy (p.106)."

That is very strong language. And I doubt that the legis-
lators who framed the laws saw it quite that way. This reminds
me of the spirit of Mary Daly's *The Church and the Second Sex*,[2]
where a strong clear feminist critique of a patriarchal institution
goes hand in hand with a still-faithful call for the turning of its
resources to the struggle for the liberation of women. The author
of that book later came to see feminist efforts to reform christian
churches as comparable to a Black person's trying to reform the
Ku Klux Klan. I find in *Sexual Harassment of Working Women*
this same tension. I cannot believe it will ever be the purpose of
any man-made law to eliminate the legal supports for male
supremacy.

Be that as it may, the book is courageous and useful. A
close look at the courts' treatment of sexual harassment helps
one understand sexual harassment and "society's" view of it.
And it must be said that the book is almost entirely free of the
blindness to race and racism and to homosexuality, lesbianism
and homophobia which have marred many of the other feminist
books of comparable importance.[3]

[1] This review was published in the *New Women's Times Feminist
Review*, Number 17, September/October 1981, pp.10-11. Another book on
sexual harassment, written in the same period, is Lin Farley, *Sexual Shake-
down: The Sexual Harassment of Women on the Job* (New York: McGraw-
Hill, 1978). [The term "sexual harassment" was coined by women around this
time; it is an example of new terminology being needed by women to name
their experience, in this case, experience that is shared by women very widely
across class, age, race, and so on, in western and westerized societies. The
existence and fairly wide adoption of this term seems to me to be a condition of
the very possibility of the Anita Hill/Clarence Thomas hearings, some 14-15
years after it was invented. 1992]

[2] New York: Harper & Row, 1968.

[3] [I do not now use "blindness" as a metaphor for ignoring or ignorance.
Such usage contributes to maintaining obnoxious prejudices about blind people
and their experience. 1992]

Re-discovering Fire[1]

A review of *Pure Lust: Elemental Feminist Philosophy,*
by Mary Daly (Boston: Beacon Press, 1984)

With *Pure Lust*, Mary Daly takes on once again that central and challenging project of a movement by women to liberate women: the work of creating new meaning. The project is challenging partly because it is "impossible"—as Alice told the rebel egg Humpty Dumpty, you can't just make words mean what you want them to mean. It is necessary because patriarchal meanings lock out the thought of woman as autonomous, yet women must be able to think themselves capable of surviving independence if they are to commit themselves to escape from servitude.

Much of Daly's work in *Pure Lust* is a scavenging through the systems of patriarchal meanings, picking up rags for a bag of semantic resources from which she and the rest of us Others can piece our new architextures of meaning. One mistake a reader can make is to reject or scorn the project if she finds Daly's own unfinished constructions displeasing to her taste or inadequate to her experience. The new meaning form, like a new art form, will arise in the different works of many creators, not by the fiat of one. Already in this book Daly's own fabrications draw much more on the works of many different women from many different places and times than does the inventing in *Gyn/Ecology* (Beacon Press, 1978); the work is thoroughly literate and for the most part very subtly responsive to criticisms and reactions feminists have brought to her earlier work. But no one thinker or artist can invent for all of us, and I find, reading *Pure Lust*, that I want it to be received as an ordinary extraordinary work. It requires and deserves our ordinary thoughtful criticism; it needs to be appreciated within a context of many women's participation in other fundamentally similar projects of meaning-making. Though they are in some cases awesome and in some cases admirable, the new pictures Daly builds in *Pure Lust* do not entirely suit me. They do inspire and encourage me to rejoin the larger project with renewed vigor, and make more pictures of my own. As for the skills of rag-picking, Daly is certainly one of the craftiest among us. There is much to learn from her methods.

Alice was right: one cannot just make words mean whatever one might want them to mean. Words, taken singly and in isolation, are meaningless; so is any sort of symbol, image, or even narrative. What has meaning means something *to* someone, and to find something meaningful is to relate it to other things and other meanings—in fact, to all other things and other meanings within one's experience. If I choose to introduce a new word, I have to define it, explicitly or implicitly, in terms of words or concepts my interlocutors already know. Novel utterances can be interpreted because they fit the patterns, the regularities, in a semantic system. (The vast majority of utterances people make are novel: exactly that sequence of words with exactly that intonation has never before been produced.) The freshest new metaphor works only because it reverberates through the existing net of meanings. "Novelty," understood as the creation of a symbol in-a-moment, out-of-nothing, never occurs. It is their connection with already-existing meanings that gives power to novel combinations.

The impossibility of arbitrary or "absolute" novelty in a culture and a symbol system underlies the meaning-making in *Gyn/Ecology* and in *Pure Lust*.

First, the Webster (one of Daly's most felicitous terms for women engaged in this enterprise) works with the elements of an existing language, in this case English, and an existing system of imagery and myth, in this case that of Euro-American christian-capitalist-commercial-scientific culture. The "new" vocabulary is made up of reassembled bits of the old; it has a certain familiar ring even as it sounds quite odd to the English-speaking ear of the woman cultured in that culture. (The "spinning voyagers" of *Gyn/Ecology* have many new names in *Pure Lust*, such as "Prudes," "Shrewds," and "Weirds.") The book is thick with dictionary definitions. Daly does not use the dictionary as an authority, but as a cultural artifact: a fairly comprehensive standard dictionary is a fairly comprehensive depository of the semantic resources for the inventions that are underway. (I have been known to complain that poets, who work with these same resources, do not have to work as hard as philosophers do because poets do not have to make everything explicit and philosophers do. My finding Daly's constant spelling out of explicit definitions somewhat tiresome is probably my punishment for such a cloddish complaint.)

Built into the project of making new meanings out of old is a political problem. For instance, some women have hoped to break through the barriers of meaning by connecting male-marked words like "judge," "officer" or "professor" with words like "woman," imagining we might generate new meanings by speaking in androgynous paradoxes. But this has yielded (in all but a few odd cases) just some not-very-new additions to the ranks of male-defined postures for women. Men have defined what positions a woman supreme court judge supports, what special value a female police officer has (she is especially good at handling domestic dispute calls and rape cases, of course), and lately, the special talent women professors have for teaching men how to "include" women in the "mainstream" curricula. Or, another example: naming God "She" or "The Great Mother." If nothing else changes, this does nothing at all but disguise the masculinity of God or heighten the pedestal on which the romanticized and hence degraded mother is confined. If the old meanings are still invoked, how can the new be radically new? Throughout this book, one of Daly's primary projects is to expose, analyze and immunize against such traps of assimilation and tokenism, against conversion to "male-ordered" "plastic feminism."

Second, patriarchal signs, symbols, images and myths were not invented out of nothing. They were constructed of the materials of an existing system. In the case of the "Western" culture which is the territory Daly is mainly working in, those earlier systems and symbols were woman-centered. The "new" patriarchal terms originally drew meaning and power from the interconnection of those symbols, which still vibrate and reverberate in, among and beneath them, even if very faintly or in layered disguise. To avoid being recaptured by phallocratic structures when we set out to make meaning, the "existing sources" we should draw on are those "original" symbols, images and myths out of which and upon which phallocratic systems have been constructed by processes of accretion, objectification, reversal, ossification, subtraction and attenuation.

If Daly's strategy can be summed up in any one word, that word is *Remember*. Her point is not that we should try to replicate some ancient matriarchy; it is that to avoid being captured in patriarchal male meanings, we should go back into their sources and backgrounds for our materials. *Pure Lust* is full of lessons in how to spot and read out the underlying or "original" semantics masked by the devices of patriarchal language, myth, image and theory. (And in the process of digging into the works of such characters as Aristotle, Aquinas, St. Paul, the popes Paul and Paul Tillich, as well as Freud and other towering figures of phallocracy, Daly provides a valuable education in "Western intellectual history" for any reader who has managed, in or out of the academy, to avoid the standard indoctrination.)

Pure Lust has three major sections which Daly calls Realms: Archespheres, Pyrospheres and Metamorphospheres. In the first of the three, she elaborates on the idea that patriarchal archetypes (she focuses especially on the Virgin Mary as the archetypical woman) are distorted and ossified constructions out of original images, those living, moving centers of meaning which she calls "Archimages" (rhymes with "rages"). One of the questions for radical feminism is this: How, if women are naturally powerful and patriarchal males are "impotent" (as Daly often says they are), could the latter ever have defeated the former? Part of the answer is given in this section, in discussions of how women are made self-defeating, self-annihilating when we buy in to the phallocratic archetypes. It is our own power that is turned against us, and this in turn helps explain why ideology, mythology and/or psychology are such large factors in the oppression of women, larger perhaps than in other sorts of oppression.

This first section ends with what was for me the single most suggestive and energizing statement in the book: "Womankind must once again dis-cover Fire." The fire in question is passion. "Pyrospheres," the second section and for me the most accessible and the most powerful, is about passion and virtue.

Systems of meaning are not abstract independent "mental" constructions. They arise with and cannot exist apart from experience. To make meaning necessarily involves new construction of the speakers and thinkers as agents; for women who have been molded in patriarchy this means getting back into motion.

On Daly's account (she draws on Aristotle and the medievals here), true passions are motions. They are natural movements toward a perceived good or away from a perceived evil. They may be "potted"—dwarfed, contained, distorted, shallow-rooted. They may also simply be replaced by "plastic" patriarchal passions or emotions which are "freefloating feelings resulting in more and more disconnectedness/fragmentation. Since they are characterized by the lack of specific and nameable causes, or 'objects' [what the emotion is about], they must be 'dealt with' endlessly in an acontextual way..."

The plastic passions she names are guilt, anxiety, depression, hostility, bitterness, resentment, frustration, boredom, resignation and fulfillment. As she says, plastic passions are endlessly preoccupying. They stiffen us into an oddly vague fixation on themselves and they fail to connect our process, as real passions would, with other people and the real world beyond themselves. They are "unnatural knots—snarls—of the spirit. Just as the fathers' lies are mind-bindings, these feelings are will-bindings that twist the movements of women's appetites upon themselves. Instead of spiraling outward, these snap backward, strangling the victim."

Daly's list and her descriptions of the plastic passions write several chapters of my own life, including some recent paragraphs on the defeats and future of radical feminism. Most particularly and vividly, she contributes to my understanding of the experience of white feminists who are caught up in an endless pseudo-struggle against racism—or rather, as we say, "around" racism.

When white feminists are blocked or "fixed" against subtle and clearheaded analysis of white "woman's place" in racism and of the racial elements of the ties than bind white women to men, we seethe with these poisonous feelings (all of Daly's list at once, except perhaps for fulfillment, with the addition of despair and panic). That these feelings do not connect any process with any reality beyond themselves and are not really passions or e-motions at all, is recognized immediately by many feminist women of color who ask us, "Where is your rage?" White women are indeed victims of implanted auto-destructive mechanisms; race works in white women's

lives as a kind of "biological determinism," constantly reinforcing our assimilation to white men; the fixation which keeps
white women from touching all of this is *designed* to separate
each of us from all other women. To Name it all might release
our rage. And the rage might liberate our "potted passions"
too, thus liberating feminist women of color from the siege of
white feminists' misdirected anger, distorted ambition and shal-
low righteousness.

In Daly's complex account of the "ultimate Taboo
against Women-Touching women," she warns against thinking
this has only to do with sexual touching, and argues that the
taboo separates women in all ways from touching ourselves and
each other. It enforces what she calls the "State of Separation"
from which radical lesbian feminists mean to separate ourselves.
I suspect that one reason white women shrink from naming and
touching racism directly is that such naming and touching is part
of what the Great Taboo forbids; it effectively precipitates white
feminists into the morass of plastic passions. The taboo against
touch may also explain why the folded-in attitude of confession
which Daly deplores has seemed to be the only possible response
to criticism of racist thinking or acting.

Daly tries to abscond with the word 'race', punning it
into a characterization of the running, spilling, rushing motion
of the metamorphosis of the "Race of Women." I imagine she
thought that grabbing the word and carrying it off like that
would work as a way of breaking its negatively charged taboo
power. I like the boldness of the move, but I do not think it
works. As she says, it is only by touching the taboo object that
we can break the spell. Her handling of the word 'race' is not the
taboo-breaking touch she wants: it seems to me to further
remove the concrete problem of race and racism—and, in another sense, women of color themselves—from the range of
white women's touch and capacity to be touched. When in *The
Politics of Reality* I tried to recast the word 'white', many of my
friends thought that what I presented as a breakout was really
only a flight. After much more work I think it is turning out that
they were wrong about that. I am quite willing to be shown by
Daly's further work that I am just as wrong to see her move with
'race' as misdirected. For now, I am not buying it.

Where other women have spoken vaguely and timidly
of "society," Daly speaks of the Phallic State, the State of

Atrocity, the State of Separation, the State of Lechery, the State of Boredom, the dismembered state, and the sadostate. The political state she would see as a logical and noxious product of the more generic state named by these phrases. The word 'state' is associated always in this work with the concept of *stasis*, the stationary, that which is not moving; all that is natural to women is characterized in terms of motion. The verb 'to be' is taken as an active verb; Daly's conception of women's being is developed entirely in terms of activities, processes, motions and movements and the qualities and modifications of motion and that which moves.

Motion may be traveling from one point to another in space, it may be change of attitude or shift of perception, it may be activity such as knitting, writing, or digging a hole. It may also be a thing's changing in such a way that it becomes a different thing than it was—a change of identity, a transformation. At the level of identity, motion is *metamorphosis*, the theme of the Third Realm, "Metamorphospheres." On Daly's account this "ontological movement" is what essentially characterizes everything that is alive, and for conscious and creative living things like us, the metaphorphosis is conscious and creative.[2] But it can take place wholly or rightly only in the environmental conditions of "statelessness." The enemies of women are individual patriots; the Enemy of Womankind and of life generally is that which impedes or stops motion. To be ourselves and not sick or dying, we must not be in a State.

Daly is consistently and wantonly anarchist. (She begins to convince me that radical feminism is essentially anarchistic.) To the believer in the state, there can be order, harmony and peace only if there is "social control," that is, force and coercion; somebody has to be in charge and that somebody has to have the power to make his decisions stick. For this belief to sound right, one has to make certain background assumptions about human and other nature (the sorts of assumptions made historically by Plato or by Hobbes). Daly does not make those assumptions, which is why her writing can seem both off-the-wall and highly impractical to some readers. Consistently with her anarchism, her worldview is both animistic and optimistic.

The universe being sounded in *Pure Lust* is conceived wholly in organic metaphors. The natural harmony Daly believes in—among women, in nature generally, and between any organism and the rest of nature—is like the harmony of the parts and functions of a healthy plant or animal. It is "natural" in the sense that it not a result of art or management—it does not require anything like our familiar, mundane and desperate striving and struggling or human-like conscious preconception and planning. It just happens; that's the way plants and animals are. So also, on a cosmic scale, harmony happens. Her world is in every way alive and active, and originally, essentially, naturally happy. Some of Daly's readers have thought her pessimistic or "negative," because of her unexpurgated analysis of the malevolence and ugliness of patriarchy, its agents and their machinations. Not so. It is the contrast between the world women experience in patriarchy and the world as she believes it might be (and in some sense is...patriarchy is "unreal") that gives her hope and makes imagination possible. She knows in her crone's bones the possibility of happiness. If it were not for that, she would not write raging and funny books but collapse in the horror of what she knows. (For the record, her analyses of the motives and means of men in power almost all seem to me mind-bogglingly right.)

In the last footnote in the book, Daly acknowledges the contributions of many other creatures—birds, butterflies, horses—who have been valuable companions to her in the course of the writing. I understand that companionship; but I have also struggled with another curriculum in the tutelage of slugs, root maggots, striped cucumber beetles, scab, mold, aphids and sturdy colonies of wild geraniums established amongst the infant carrots. Working in our garden, we fertilize and barricade, spray and sprinkle, disperse purely organic poisons and "biological controls," and with our fingers squash or rip out small beings whose identities are not known but who look to an educated eye like suspicious characters. All this in our efforts to preserve from predation and fatal competition what is to be a significant part of our supply of relatively unpolluted food for the year. As we work, acquiring in the process nasty sunburns and mosquito bites which will harass us out of our rest at night, my lover and I have been known ironically to incant the syllables *bi-o-phil-i-a* to the tune of the Hallelujah Chorus. These experiences provoke my chariness about Daly's concepts of *natural, biophilic, wild* and *real*, as indeed some of my experience of friendship among women has also done. Certain kinds and degrees of enthusiasms are not possible for me, even though my bones too sometimes speak of happiness.

At some points in the development of life on this planet some human animals entered a kind of existence in which concepts like *weed* and *pest* had application, and in which human bodies were tortured regularly by the work of tillage, human livelihoods threatened by two more days with or without rain. Now most of us who have the time and will to philosophize subsist on food produced by the tortured labor of other miserably exploited people and with the aid of tons of dangerous chemicals. How are we to imagine feeing and sheltering all of us without exploiting any of us, and without engaging in that perilous struggle with nature which is agriculture and horticulture? We cannot become a planet of communities of hunter-gatherers migrating through territories abundant with the food and weather we need. The point is not that fructarian grazing is the only correct and "biophilic" way to eat. What bothers me is that I don't have a useful, practical, ordinary understanding of "love of life" or of that "harmony" in which we want to be with plants and planets and with other animals—including each other.

I do not believe Daly's anarchic harmony is natural in the sense of requiring no straining and no deliberate invention. I merely believe it is possible. That sets for me the tasks of figuring out how to love life, how to understand the fact that in nature living things kill and eat other living things all the time, how to behave honorably, virtuously when another's vital motion would block mine—or mine hers—*et cetera*.

In *Pure Lust*, Mary Daly's contribution to such work is indirect. It comes in the form of exemplary iconoclasm (the shattering of the concept of *species*, for instance, is music to my ears), lessons in method that are more like art lessons than cooking lessons (no recipes are given), a prodigious new profusion of metaphors for mixing into conceptions of ourselves, and the renewing encouragement of Daly's own terrific vitality and inventiveness.

[1] This review was published in *The New Women's Review of Books*, Vol.1, No.11, August 1984.

[2] This may provide the answer to the conundrum given by Carol Anne Douglas in her review of *Pure Lust* in *off our backs* (June, 1984), as to how Daly can be both an essentialist and an existentialist, both of which she seems to be.

Making Worlds of Sense

Lesbian 'Sex'[1]

1987

The reasons the word 'sex' is in quotation marks in my title are two: one is that the term 'sex' is an inappropriate term for what lesbians do, and the other is that whatever it is that lesbians do that (for lack of a better word) might be called 'sex' we apparently do damned little of it. For a great many lesbians, the gap between the high hopes we had some time ago for lesbian sex and the way things have worked out has turned the phrase 'lesbian sex' into something of a bitter joke. I don't want to exaggerate: many lesbians are having gratifying erotic lives. But in our communities as a whole, there is much grumbling about "lesbian bed death," especially in long-term relationships.[2] I want to explore the meanings of the relative dearth of what (for lack of a better word) we call lesbian 'sex.' These meanings connect in interesting ways with other aspects of the feminist discussion of what (for lack of a better word) we call "sexuality," and "sexuality" is clearly very significant in the webs of meaning and force which keep patriarchy going.

Recent discussions of lesbian "sex" frequently cite the findings of a study on couples by Blumstein and Schwartz[3] which is perceived by most of those who discuss it as having been done well, with a good sample of couples—lesbian, male homosexual, heterosexual non-married and heterosexual married couples. These people apparently found that lesbian couples "have sex" far less frequently than any other type of couple, that lesbians couples are less "sexual" as couples and as individuals than anyone else. In their sample, only about one third of lesbians in relationships of two years or longer "had sex" once a week or more; 47% of lesbians in long term relationships "had sex" once a month or less, while among heterosexual married couples only 15% had sex once a month or less. And they report that lesbians seem to be more limited in the range of their "sexual" techniques than are other couples.

When this sort of information first came into my circle of lesbian friends, we tended to see it as conforming to what we know from our own experience. We were not surprised to hear that we "had" less "sex" than anyone else or that in our long-term relationships we "had sex" a great deal less frequently than other sorts of couples. This seemed to pretty much fit our knowledge of ourselves and of each other. But on more reflection, and looking again at what has been going on with us in our long-term relationships, the nice fit between this report and our experience seemed not so perfect after all.

It was brought to our attention during our ruminations on this that what 85% of long-term heterosexual married couples do more than once a month takes on the average 8 minutes to do.[4]

Although in my experience lesbians discuss their "sex" lives with each other relatively little (a point to which I will return), I know from my own experience and from the reports of a few other lesbians in long-term relationships, that what we do that, on average, we do considerably less frequently, takes on the average, considerably more than 8 minutes to do. Maybe about 30 minutes at the least. Sometimes maybe about an hour. And it is not uncommon that among these relatively uncommon occurrences, an entire afternoon or evening is given over to activities organized around doing it. The suspicion arises that what 85% of heterosexual married couples are doing more than once a month and what 47% of lesbians couples are doing less than once a month is not the same thing. And if they are not doing the same thing, how was this research done that would line these different things up against each other to compare how many times they were done?

I remember that one of my first delicious tastes of old gay lesbian culture occurred in a bar where I was chatting with some other lesbians I was just getting acquainted with. One was talking about being busted out of the Marines for being gay. She had been put under suspicion somehow, and was sent off to the base psychiatrist to be questioned, her perverted tendencies to be assessed. He wanted to convince her she had only been engaged in a little youthful experimentation and wasn't really gay. To this end, he questioned her about the extent of her experience. What he asked was, "How many times have you had sex with a woman?" At this, we all laughed and giggled: what an ignorant fool he was! What does he think he means by "times"? What will we count? What's to *count*?

Another of my friends years later, discussing the same conundrum, said that she thought maybe every time you got up to go to the bathroom, that marked a "time." The joke about "how many times" is still good for a chuckle from time to time in my life with my lover. I have no memory of any such topic providing any such merriment in my years of sexual encounters and relationships with men. It would have been very rare indeed that we would not have known how to answer the question "How many times did you do it?"

If what heterosexual married couples do that the individuals report under the rubric "sex" or "have sex" is something that in most instances can easily be individuated into countable instances, this is more evidence that it is not what long-term lesbian couples do...or, for that matter, what short-term lesbian couples do.[5]

What violence did the lesbians do their experience by answering the same question the heterosexuals answered, as though it had the same meaning for them? How did the lesbians figure out how to answer the questions "How frequently?" or "How many times?" My guess is, for starters, that different individuals figured it out differently, to some degree. Some might have counted a two or three-cycle evening as one "time" they "had sex"; some might have counted that as two or three "times." Some may have counted as "times" only the times both partners had orgasms; some may have counted as "times" occasions on which at least one had an orgasm; some may not have orgasms or have them rarely and may not have figured orgasms into the calculations; perhaps they counted as a "time" every episode in which both touched the other's vulva more than fleetingly and not for something like a health examination. For some, to count every reciprocal touch of the vulva would have made them count as "having sex" more than most people with work to do would dream of having time for; how do we suppose those individuals counted "times"? Is there any good reason why they should not count all those as "times"? Does it depend on how fulfilling it was? (Was anybody else counting by occasions of fulfillment?)

We have no idea how individual lesbians individuated their so-called "sexual acts" or encounters; we have no idea what it means when they said they did it less than once a month. But this raises questions for how the heterosexuals individuated and counted *their* sexual acts or encounters. I think many lesbians, when pressed to answer a question like "How many times a month do you have sex?" count times both partners had orgasms. That seems to them definitive enough. Did the heterosexuals who responded to these questions count only the times both parties had orgasms? Did the men count all the times they had orgasms, and the women count all the times they had orgasms? If so, one would expect the authors of the study to have noted a considerable difference between the reports of the women and of the men in the samples of heterosexual couples. In my experience, and by my reading of the predominant culture generally heterosexual pairs count as having had sex whether the woman had an orgasm or not. And in my experience and by my reading of the culture at large, heterosexual pairs might not count themselves as having had sex if all that was done was the man digitally stimulated the woman's clitoris until she had an orgasm. I think that if the heterosexual women counted "times" according to the standard meaning of "have sex" in English, they counted not according to their own experience of orgasm or even arousal, but according to their partners' orgasms and ejaculations. One wonders how heterosexual women would have individuated and counted the incidents of "having sex" in their relationships if they had not counted according to their partners' orgasms and ejaculations, or how they did count "times" if they did not count them this way. If the havings of sex by heterosexual married couples did take on the average 8 minutes, my guess is that in a large number of those cases the women did not experience orgasms. My guess is that neither the women's pleasure nor the women's orgasms were pertinent in most of the individuals' counting and reporting the frequency with which they "had sex."

So, do lesbian couples really "have sex" any less frequently than heterosexual couples? My own view is that lesbian couples "have sex" a great deal less frequently than heterosexual couples: I think, in fact, we don't "have sex" at all. By the criteria that I'm betting most of the heterosexual people used in reporting the frequency with which they have sex, lesbians don't have sex. There is no male partner whose orgasm and ejaculation can be the criterion for counting "times." (I'm willing to draw the conclusion that heterosexual women don't have sex either, that what they report is the frequency with which their partners had sex.)

I t has been said before by feminists that the concept of "having sex" is a phallic concept; that it pertains to heterosexual intercourse, in fact, primarily to heterosexist intercourse, that is, male-dominant-female-subordinate-copulation-whose-completion-and-purpose-is-the-male's-ejaculation. I have thought this was true since the first time the idea was put to me, some 12 years ago.[6] But I have been finding lately that I have to go back over some of the ground I covered a decade ago because some of what I knew then I knew too superficially. For some of us, myself included, the move from heterosexual relating to lesbian relating was occasioned or speeded up or brought to closure by our recognition that what we had done under the heading "having sex" had indeed been male-dominant-female-subordinate-copulation-whose-completion-and-purpose-is-the-male's-ejaculation, and it was not worthy of doing. Yet now, years later, we are willing to answer questionnaires that ask us how frequently we "have sex," and are dissatisfied with ourselves and with our relationships because we don't "have sex" enough. We are so dissatisfied that we keep a small army of therapists in business trying to help us "have sex" more.

We quit having sex years ago, and for excellent and compelling reasons. What exactly is our complaint now?

In all these years I've been doing and writing feminist theory, I have not until very recently written, much less published, a word about sex. I did not write, though it was suggested to me that I do so, anything in the SM debates; I left entirely unanswered an invitation to be the keynote speaker at a feminist conference about women's sexuality (which by all reports turned out to be an excellent conference). I was quite unable to think of anything but vague truisms to say, and very few of those. Feminist theory is grounded in experience; I have always written feminist political and philosophical analysis from the bottom up, starting with my own encounters and adventures, frustrations, pain, anger, etc. (Sometimes it has ended up, no doubt partly because of this, a little provincial; but it has at least had the virtue of firm connection with someone's real life experience, which is more than you can say for a lot of philosophy, including a lot of feminist theory.) When I put to myself the task of theorizing about sex and sexuality, it was as though I had no experience, as though there was no ground on which and from which to generate theory. But, if I understand the terminology rightly, I have in fact been what they call "sexually active" for close to a quarter of a century, about half my life, almost all of what they call one's "adult life," heterosexually, lesbianly, and "autoerotically." Surely I have experience. But I seem not to have experiential knowledge of the sort I need.

Reflecting on all that history, I realize that in many of its passages this experience has been a muddle. Acting, being acted on, choosing, desiring, pleasure and displeasure all akimbo—not coherently determining each other. Even in its greatest intensity it has for the most part been somehow rather opaque to me, not fully in my grasp. My "experience" has in general the character more of a buzzing blooming confusion than of experience. And it has occurred in the midst of almost total silence on the part of others about their experience. The experience of others has for the most part also been opaque to me; they do not discuss or describe it in detail at all.

I recall an hours-long and heated argument among some eight or ten lesbians at a party a couple of years ago about SM, whether it is okay, or not. When Carolyn and I left, she noted that in the whole time not one woman had said one concrete, explicit, physiologically specific thing about what she actually did. The one arguing in favor of bondage: Did she have her hands tied gently with ribbons or scarves, or harshly with handcuffs or chains? What other parts of her body were or weren't restrained, and by what means? And what parts of her body were touched, and how, while she was bound? And what liberty did she still have to touch in return? And if she had no such liberty, was it part of her experience to want that liberty and experience tension or frustration, or was it her experience that she felt pleased or satisfied not to have that liberty...? Who knows? She never said a single word at this level of specificity. Nor did anyone else, pro or con.

I once perused a large and extensively illustrated book on sexual activity by and for homosexual men. It was astounding to me for one thing in particular, namely, that its pages constituted a huge lexicon of specific vocabulary: words for acts and activities, their sub-acts, preludes and denouements, their stylistic variation, their sequences. Gay male sex, I realized then, is articulate. It is articulate to a degree that, in my world, lesbian "sex" does not remotely approach. Lesbian "sex" as I have known it most of the time I have known it is utterly inarticulate. Most of my lifetime, most of my experience in the realms commonly designated as "sexual" has been pre-linguistic, non-cognitive. I have, in effect, no linguistic community, no language, and therefore in one important sense, no knowledge.

In situations of male dominance, women are a "muted" group inasmuch as women are for the most part excluded from the formulation and validation of meaning and thereby denied the means to express themselves. Men's meanings, and no women's meanings, are encoded in what is presumed to be the whole population's language. (In many cases, both the men and the women assume it is everyone's language.) The meanings one's life and experience can generate cannot come fully into operation without being encoded: they are fleeting, or they hover, vague, not fully coalesced, not *useful* for explaining or grounding interpretations, desires, complaints, theories. In response to our understanding that there is something going on in patriarchy that is more-or-less well described by saying women's meanings are not encoded in the dominant languages and that this keeps our experience from being fully formed and articulate, we have undertaken quite deliberately to discover, complete and encode our meanings. Such simple things as naming chivalrous gestures "insulting," naming Virginia Woolf a great writer, naming ourselves women instead of girls or ladies. Coining terms like 'sexism', 'sexual harassment' and 'incestor'. Mary Daly's *Wickedary*[7] is a whole project of "encoding" meanings, and we can all find examples of our own more local encodings.[8]

Meanings should arise from our bodily self-knowledge,

bodily play, tactile communication, the ebb and flow of intense excitement, arousal, tension, release, comfort, discomfort, pain and pleasure (and I make no distinctions here among bodily, emotional, intellectual, aesthetic). But such meanings are more completely muted, less coalesced into discrete elements of a coherent pattern of meanings (of an experience) than any other dimensions of our lives. In fact, there are for many of us virtually no meanings in this realm because nothing of it is crystallized in a linguistic matrix.[9]

What we have for generic words to cover this terrain are the words 'sex', 'sexual' and 'sexuality'. In our efforts to liberate ourselves from the stifling woman-hating Victorian denial that women even have bodily awareness, arousal, excitement, orgasms and so on, many of us actively took these words for ourselves, and claimed that we do "do sex" and we are sexual and we have sexuality. This has been particularly important to lesbians because the very fact of 'sex' being a phallocentric term has made it especially difficult to get across the idea that lesbians are not, for lack of a penis between us [as Alix Dobkin put it in a song lyric], making do with feeble and partial and pathetic half-satisfactions. (Asserting the robustness and unladylikeness of our passions and actions, some of us have called some of what we do "fucking.") But it seems to me that the attempt to encode our lustiness and lustfulness, our passion and our vigorous carnality in the words 'sex', 'sexual' and 'sexuality' has backfired. Instead of losing their phallocentricity, these words have imported the phallocentric meanings into and onto experience which is not in any way phallocentric. A web of meanings which maps emotional intensity, excitement, arousal, bodily play, orgasm, passion and relational adventure back onto a semantic center in male-dominant-female-subordinate-copulation-whose-completion-and-purpose-is-the-male's-ejaculation has been so utterly inadequate as to leave us speechless, meaningless, and ironically, according to the Blumstein and Schwartz report, "not as sexual" as couples or as individuals as any other group.

Our lives, the character of our embodiment, cannot be mapped back on to that semantic center. When we try to synthesize and articulate it by the rules of that mapping, we end up trying to mold our loving and passionate carnal intercourse into explosive 8-minute events. But that is the timing and the ontology of an alienated and patriarchal penis, not of the lesbian body. When the only things that count as "doing it" are those passages of our interactions which most closely approximate a paradigm that arose from the meanings of the rising and falling penis, no wonder we discover ourselves to "do it" rather less often than do pairs with one or more penises present. Interpreting our desires and determining our acts by the rules of that semantic map, we have tended to discount, discontinue, never try, or never even imagine acts, activities, practices, rituals, forms of play, ways of touching, looking, talking, which might be woven into a fabric of our erotic experience.

There are many cultural and social-psychological reasons why women (in white Euro-American groups, but also in many other configurations and realizations of patriarchy) would generally be somewhat less clear and less assertive about their desires and about getting their satisfactions than men would generally be. And when we pair up two women in a couple, it stands to reason that those reasons would double up and tend to effect relationships in which there is a lowish frequency of clearly delineated desires and direct initiations of satisfactions. But for all the help it might be to lesbian bodies to work past the psychological and behavioral habits of femininity that inhibit our passions and pleasures, my suggestion is that what we have never taken seriously enough is the language which mutes our meanings.

My positive recommendation is this: Instead of starting with a point (a point in the life of a body unlike our own) and trying to make meanings along vectors from that point, we would do better to start with a wide field of our passions and bodily pleasures and make meanings that weave a web across it. I suggest that we begin the creation of a vocabulary that can encode and expand our meanings by adopting a very wide and general concept of "doing it." Let it be an open, generous, commodious concept encompassing all the acts and activities by which we generate with each other and thrills, tenderness and ecstacy, passages of passionate carnality of whatever duration or profundity. Everything from vanilla to licorice, from puce to tangerine, from velvet to ice, from cuddles to cunts, from chortles to tears. Starting from there, we can let our experiences generate a finer-tuned descriptive vocabulary that maps and expresses the differences and distinctions among the things we do, the kinds of pleasures we get, the stages and styles of our acts and activities, the parts of our bodies centrally engaged in the different kinds of "doing it," and so on. Our vocabulary will arise among us as we explain and explore and define our pleasures and our preferences across this field, teaching each other what the possibilities are and how to make them real.

The vocabulary will arise among us, of course, only if we talk with each other about what we're doing and why, and what it feels like. Language is social. So is "doing it."

I'm hoping it will be a lot easier to talk about what we do, and how and when and why, concretely and in detail, once we've learned to laugh at foolish studies that show that lesbians don't have sex as often as, aren't as sexual as and use fewer sexual techniques than other folks.

[1] This essay was first published in *Sinister Wisdom*, vol. 35 (Summer/Fall 1988). It was first presented as a paper at the meeting of the Society for Women in Philosophy, Midwestern Division, November 13-15, 1987. It was occasioned by Claudia Card's paper "What Lesbian Do," which was published under the title "Intimacy and Responsibility: What Lesbians Do," as the Institute for Legal Studies, University of Wisconsin-Madison Law School Working Papers Series 2, No. 10. Carolyn Shafer has contributed a lot to my thinking here, and I am indebted also to conversations with Sue Emmert and Terry Grant. For more writing by lesbians on sex, see *An Intimate Wilderness: Lesbian Writers on Sexuality*, edited by Judith Barrington (Portland, OR: Eighth Mountain Press, 1991).

[2] When I speak of "we" and "our communities," I actually don't know exactly who that is. I know only that such issues are being discussed in my own circles and in communities other than mine as well (as witness, e.g., discussion in the pages of the *Lesbian Connection*). If what I say here resonates for you, so be it. If not, at least you can know it resonates for some range of lesbians and some of them probably are your friends or acquaintances.

[3] Philip Blumstein and Pepper Schwartz, *American Couples* (NY: William Morrow and Company, 1983).

[4] Dotty Calabrese gave this information in her workshop on long-term lesbian relationships at the Michigan Womyn's Music Festival, 1987. (Thanks to Terry Grant for this reference.)

[5] In their questionnaire, Blumstein and Schwartz use the term "have sexual relations." In the text of their book, they use "have sex."

[6] It was brought to my attention by Carolyn Shafer. See pp. 156-7 of my book *The Politics of Reality* (Freedom, CA: The Crossing Press, 1983).

[7] *Websters' First New Intergalactic Wickedary of the English Language* (Boston: Beacon Press, 1987).

[8] I use the word 'encoding' as it is used in the novel *Native Tongue*, by Suzette Haden Elgin (NY: Daw Books, Inc., 1984). She envisages women

identifying concepts, feelings, types of situations, etc., for which there are no words in English (or any other language), and giving them intuitively appropriate names in a women-made language called Laadan.

⁹ Carolyn Shafer has speculated that one significant reason why lesbian SM occasioned so much excitement, both positive and negative, is that lesbians have been starved for language—for specific, detailed, literal, particular, bodily talk with clear non-metaphorical references to parts of our bodies and the ways they can be stimulated, to acts, postures, types of touch. Books about SM like *Coming to Power* (Boston: Alyson Publications, 1982) feed that need, and call forth more words in response.

Lesbian Community: Heterodox Congregation[1]

1989

(On Saturday, April 29, 1989 at the Mountainmoving Coffeehouse in Chicago, I was a member of a panel of nine lesbians who had contributed to the new anthology *For Lesbians Only*[2], a collection of lesbian separatist writings. Each of us did a reading or made a short presentation. This is the statement I composed and read for the occasion.)

I live in Lansing, Michigan. I have lived there for almost 15 years. There's a lesbian community there which I, along with many others, have worked to create, grow and maintain. This community has been shaped in many ways by lesbians who are separatist—though being separatist does not mean the same thing to all of us. I'm proud of the lesbian community in the town I live in. I move in that community with a strong and satisfying sense of shared accomplishments. I want to talk a bit about that community tonight.

Two things have happened recently in my community that have generated a lot of feeling and a lot of talk. The two things weren't causally connected with each other; they just happened to happen close to each other. About a week ago, a lesbian in my town committed suicide. She did it decisively and deliberately. The other thing is that Sarah Hoagland's recent presentation in Lansing triggered open conflict about the value of 12-step programs to individual dykes and as an influence in the community. Both of these things, the suicide and the conflict, focussed my attention on lesbian community—what it is, how it works, what kind of glue holds it together.

Probably the most obvious thing about what makes this community a community is that it is *not* that we agree on everything. There is, in fact, much disagreement on practically everything. Here's a list of some things there is *not* agreement on in my community:

- we do not agree on the importance of recycling jars and paper, or on whether it's okay to have christmas trees;
- we do not agree about what the priority is on working against US imperialism in Central America or on working against nuclear power & nuclear weapons, or on working for legal and available abortions;
- we do not agree on whether the practice of friend-ship requires remaining supportive, or even civil, to lesbians who go straight, or requires active support of lesbians who have male babies;
- we all say that we are against racism, but we do not agree at all about what it is or what to do about it;
- we don't agree about whether it's ok to wear skirts and dresses, to shave our legs, to get permanents, to wear make-up; we don't agree about whether 12-step programs are wholesome for dykes, or whether it's okay to practice or to purchase therapy;
- we do not agree about how much of the Lesbian Alliance's funds should be donated to the Sharon Kowalski fund, or about whether the Lesbian Alliance and the Ambitous Amazons should try to work together more;
- we don't agree about what kinds of behavior be-tween lovers are okay and what kinds are ter-rible;
- we do not agree about whether there is still any such thing women's music or about whether the Olivia Caribbean cruises are absurd;
- we don't agree about how important it is to have events, activities and homes accessible to wheel

chair users, or about whether it's ok to drink
alcohol, to go to weddings, to like your father or
brother, to de-dyke your house when your parents visit, to get a hot-tub or a nice car if you can
afford it, to watch tv, or to go to a male dentist;
• we do not agree about hamburgers.

And this is only a few of the things we don't all agree about
in my community. I'm sure I don't even know what some of the
things are that we don't agree about.

You might suppose that there is agreement among us on
some other level, and I supposed it too. But the issues about 12-
step programs have made me doubt it. I thought that in spite of
all our differences about specific actions and practices, what
held us together was something some of us have called "ethical
compatibility"—some deep likeness of ethical and political intuition. I have thought something like that underlay our *lesbianism*, our *desire* for each other. But now I'm thinking that within
my community there is not even a significant likeness of basic
ethical and political intuition.

So what *is* there? What holds us in community? The
answer seems to be either (1) nothing holds us in community, or
(2) I've asked the wrong question. I opt for (2).

What I'm getting at here is that it's the natural normal
thing for women to be connected and sustained in community
with each other, and it has nothing in particular to do with
agreeing about anything, or even liking each other. It certainly
doesn't have anything in particular to do with approving of each
other. Instead of looking for something like common values to
account for what holds us together, we should consider whatever kept us apart or works to keep us apart... And this brings
me to the topic of separatism.

Heteropatriarchal forms of social organization keep
women apart from women, separate women from women. And
that, I would say, is unnatural. I spoke at the beginning of
creating and maintaining lesbian community. But when I think
about the actual activities and behaviors we do, what they
mostly add up to is not *building* something, but just *clearing
space* for something. Almost all the organizing adds up to
nothing more than making space and getting a whole bunch of
lesbians in that space all at once. That is, we separate lesbians
from separation from each other and then community happens.

It is anarchic, often strife-ridden and stressful, not always fun, not always affirming of whatever we think about things or about ourselves, but it's also just the normal thing for women—to be in lesbian connection with each other. It doesn't have to be explained.

Now, what about the suicide? It is terribly sad and awful, and I grieve for the life that might have been. It makes everyone wonder what we could or should have done to make living tolerable, not to mention joyful, for that woman. But one of my friends (with whom I disagree about some very important things) noted that in the almost fifteen years we've known this community of many hundreds of lesbians, this is only the second suicide she knew of (only the first that I had known of). Before the current era of lesbian feminist consciousness and gay rights, suicide was epidemic among lesbians, so my older friends have told me. But it is not, among us. In the time I have known this community, we have fought and quarrelled, and trashed, and bashed, and made love and made hate, had parties and played and flowed through shifting patterns of affiliation and ostracism, and had powerful feelings of solidarity and powerful feelings of alienation from each other, and put out a zillion newsletters and fliers and organized fund-raisers and gossiped, and felt great and felt terrible. And lesbians in my community have survived in large numbers.

What I'm saying is that lesbian community is possible—a community that is "separate" in the sense that there is a lesbian center of gravity (or of hilarity, perhaps), a force field, in which natural lesbian connection happens, which sustains and protects lesbians in many ways and varying degrees from the ravages of misogyny and heterosexualism, even, for some and in some ways from the violences of racism and poverty.

In my community, lesbians don't agree about anything and **lesbians survive in droves.**

---

[1] This talk was published in the magazine *Lesbian Ethics*, Vol.4, No.1, Spring 1990.

[2] *For Lesbian Only: A Separatist Anthology*, edited by Julia Penelope and Sarah Lucia Hoagland (London: Onlywomen Press, 1988).

Willful Virgin or Do You Have to Be a Lesbian to Be a Feminist?[1]

1990

The connection between lesbianism and feminism has made many women nervous. Many believe that if they associate themselves with feminism they will be associated with lesbianism, and for some that is a frightening, even a disgusting, thought. There is fear of being suspected of approving of lesbians or lesbianism, fear of being identified with lesbians, fear of being suspected of being a lesbian, fear of being lesbian. And there is anger at lesbians for being present, active and assertive as feminists, and for insisting on a connection between lesbianism and feminism.

I will directly provoke and address these fears and this anger here. They are homophobic, more specifically, *gyn*ophobic and lesbian-hating, and they make me impatient. I am going to speak plainly, out of impatience and also out of my own peculiar and slightly perverse optimism.

Every term in my feminism classes, a time comes when heterosexual women students articulate the question: Do you have to be a lesbian to be a feminist? I don't know how much other teachers of Women's Studies hear this question. My classroom is a situation which brings the connection between feminism and lesbianism to one's attention. I am a lesbian, I am "out" to my Women's Studies students, and I expose them to a great deal of strong and empowering feminist thinking by feminists of many cultures and locales who are lesbians. In the classroom, this question signals our arrival at a point where newcomers to feminism are beginning to grasp that sexual acts, sexual desire, and sexual dread and taboo are profoundly political and that feminist politics is as much about the disposition of bodies, the manipulation of desire and arousal, and the bonds of intimacy and loyalty as it is about gender stereotypes, economic opportunity and legal rights. In my classes, this question is a moment of students' coming to terms with the fact that the political is indeed personal, very personal. But what goes on in my class is clearly not the only thing that gives rise to this question. For many students it has already arisen outside this class; they have elsewhere encountered people who apparently believe that if you are a feminist you must be a lesbian. Some students have been just waiting for the chance to pose this question. I usually ask women in my Women's Studies classes if they have ever been called lesbians or dykes or been accused of being lesbian, and always many, often a majority, say they have. One woman was called a lesbian when she rejected the attentions of a man in a bar; another was called "butch" when she opened and held a door for a male friend; another was asked if she was a lesbian when she challenged a man's sexist description of another woman. A woman told her date that she did not want to have sex with him and he called her a dyke. A young woman told her mother that she was going to Washington D.C. for the big pro-choice march; her mother, disapproving and fearing for her daughter's safety, said, "Oh, so now you're going to go off and become a lesbian." A woman who divorced her husband and lives on her own is gossiped about in a way that spreads the suggestion that she is a lesbian. A woman says she is frequently assumed to be a lesbian because of her athletic build and refusal to wear skirts. A woman who does not experience sexual arousal or orgasm with her husband is quizzed about her lesbian tendencies by her doctor and her therapist. A woman reports that her friends refer to her Women's Studies class as her "lesbian class"; several other women say some of their friends do that too.

The message of these exchanges is clearly that a woman who is feminist or does anything or betrays any attitude or desire which expresses her autonomy or deviance from conventional femininity is a lesbian. Hearing this message in these contexts, women are likely to "consider the source"—the message has come from people who are anti-feminist, misogynist or at least unreflective defenders of male privilege or the gender status quo. One might think they are inventing this equation just to intimidate women who are "out of line." But it is more complicated than that. These are not the only people who suggest to newly feminist women that they can't be feminists without being lesbians. Paradoxically, some heterosexual feminists suggest the same thing to them in many ways. Consider what may go on, what often does go on, in the context of Women's Studies in universities and colleges.

In a Women's Studies program somewhere in the U.S. students register with the Women's Studies advisory committee the complaint that their courses are not challenging and radical enough, and a key faculty member surmises that the students who are dissatisfied are lesbian. The dissatisfied students, few of whom are lesbian, pick up on this response, and those who are not lesbian learn that they are out of step because they want their radicalness and rebellion nurtured and they are not lesbian.

Another example: Some students who have been exposed to the thinking and lives of feminist lesbians bring ideas from there into a Women's Studies course and those ideas are denigrated by that teacher, who identifies them as ideas only a lesbian separatist would consider. Some of those students are not lesbian and yet they have considered those ideas and found them interesting, even compelling, and have found themselves empowered just by thinking about those ideas. They are being told these ideas belong to lesbians, and heterosexual women don't believe those things or even take them seriously.

In many Women's Studies contexts, students are exposed to heterosexual feminist teachers (and sometimes closeted lesbian teachers who are passing as heterosexuals) who model conformity to man-made norms of femininity in appearance, bearing and voice, who argue against any action or politics that would alienate men or non-feminist women, who do not model, approve, or encourage any radical insubordination, any blasphemy against men and their gods, any uncareful enactment of anger. In academic settings it is common that women see these things modeled, hear the violences of men against women unqualifiedly named and condemned, and hear witty mockery of men's arrogances, only by feminists who are lesbian—usually students, more rarely, teachers.

In colleges and universities in the U.S. there is now, after 20 years of hard work, a great deal of feminist knowledge and analysis available to students and there are many students eagerly acquiring a rich understanding of women's subordination in U.S. cultures. Students who are exposed to the well-known data on wife-battering, street rape and acquaintance rape, pornography, child sexual assault, incest and other violences against women, and to any deep and acute feminist analysis of the patriarchal structures of marriage, reproduction and mothering—students who are exposed to feminist analyses of patriarchal religions and of the mythology propagated by popular culture in contemporary societies—students who understand something about women's paid and unpaid work in various modern economies and the practices and institutions which determine the accumulation and distribution of wealth—students who have some idea of the scope and intent of historical conspiracies against women such as the Inquisition, the erasure of women from history, and the post-World War II propaganda campaign in the U.S. to convert women workers into housewife-consumers—such students catch on that what we are dealing with here is profound, that it goes to the root of this society and what is called "civilization" and is etched into the deepest sources of our own thoughts and passions. They get it that any adequate response to this is going to require radical analysis, radical strategies and radical imagination, and that rebellion will be dangerous and costly. Feminists in the academy have helped students to appreciate the character and magnitude of the problems; students then look to these feminists for resources for responding to the problems—intellectual, spiritual, artistic, emotional, political resources. But when they express this need they often are told, either implicitly or explicitly, that only lesbians crave radical analysis and radical solutions and that only lesbians offer these. They are being told that a strong and angry feminism that will settle for nothing but going to the root of the matter belongs to lesbians. Heterosexual women associated with Women's Studies to a great extent leave the whole task of "being radical" to lesbians, leave the burden, the hopefulness and the excitement of pushing the limits to lesbians. They leave rage and ecstasy to lesbians.

In a variety of contexts, newly feminist women find their assertions and demands met with this implicit or explicit connecting of sexuality and politics. It is a sort of implicit theory of women's sexuality according to which a woman who largely adheres to patriarchal feminine norms in act and attitude and who does not radically challenge or rebel against patriarchal institutions is heterosexual, and a woman who does not comply with feminine norms or who seriously challenges or rebels against patriarchal institutions is a lesbian. The difference between the explicit accusations of lesbianism on the part of non- or anti-feminists and the implicit association of feminist radicalness with lesbianism that occurs in many academic contexts is only a difference in the degree and kind of non-compliance it takes to earn the attributed status of lesbian. Feminists are, by definition, to some degree non-compliant with the patriarchal norms of femininity and rebellious against patriarchal institutions; so by this theory, feminists are to some degree lesbian. It would follow that those who are *very* feminist, *uncompromisingly* feminist, *extremely* feminist, *radically* feminist, must BE lesbians, flat out.

For the newly feminist woman who is not lesbian, this connecting of feminism (or any sign of female autonomy or rebellion) with lesbianism is very likely to have the effect of making her back off from any radicalness, censor in herself any extremeness of anti-patriarchal thought or action. She has lived all her life in a social climate that makes lesbianism scary and offensive and that makes her believe she herself is not and could never be lesbian. If she is a member of a racialized group, she may also have some sense that to be a lesbian would be disloyal to her home community, or she may have the impression that lesbianism simply does not occur among her people. In such contexts, the equation of feminism and lesbianism is a very effective way to place a very narrow and constraining limit on feminism.

But even though the linking of feminism and lesbianism actually does work—in conjunction with women's homophobia and lesbian-hating—to restrain feminism, and even though our contemporary concept of lesbianism is rooted in theories of sexuality which were invented in a period of fearful and extreme reaction against 19th century feminism, I want to suggest that this notion of a connection between feminism and lesbianism is *not* merely an *ad hoc* fiction invented by patriarchal loyalists to vilify feminism and intimidate feminists. An intrinsic connection between feminism and lesbianism in a contemporary Euro-American setting is just a historically specific manifestation of an ancient and intrinsic connection between patriarchal/fraternal social order and female heterosexuality.

I believe that all feminist theory and practice eventually conveys one to this proposition: that a central constitutive dynamic and key mechanism of the global phenomenon of male domination, oppression and exploitation of females, is near-universal female heterosexuality. All of the institutions and practices which constitute and materialize this domination (and simultaneously organize males' lives in relation to each other) either presuppose almost-universal female heterosexuality or manufacture, regulate and enforce female heterosexuality, or both.

In saying this, I am using a term, "heterosexuality," which has a particular meaning in contemporary Euro-American cultures and does not translate in any simple way into other cultural contexts. In some cultures the physical intimacy between women which we here think of as central to the concept *lesbian* are not tabooed as they are here—they may not be socially recognized at all, even negatively.[2] But in almost all cultures for at least the last couple of thousand years, to the best of my knowledge, virtually every woman is strenuously required by tradition, law, more and taboo to be in some form of availability, servitude or marriage to a man or men in which she is unconditionally or almost unconditionally sexually accessible to that man or men and in the context of which she carries and bears his or their children. In cultures most shaped by male domination, wives' (females slaves', or servants') compulsory sexual accessibility and service is of a piece with their economic and domestic service and subordination to the man or men to whom they are attached and in some cases to those men's whole fraternity, family or clan.[3] Even though, in many cultures a distinction between two female sexualities, "hetero-" and "lesbian," is not operative, my use of the term "heterosexual" is suitable because I am referring to life-situations and dispositions of female bodies which are defined and determined in terms of female sexual accessibility to males and not in terms of the whole of a female's *own* desire, affectional ties or erotic intimacies, whatever their objects. The point is that virtually all women in patriarchal cultures are rigorously required to be sexual with and for men. When I speak of "the patriarchal institution of female heterosexuality" and suggest that in some sense "it" exists widely across cultures and time, I speak of a nearly global pattern using a term which strictly designates just one of its local manifestations.[4]

For females to be subordinated and subjugated to males on a global scale, and for males to organize themselves and each other as they do, billions of female individuals, virtually all who see life on this planet, must be reduced to a more-or-less willing toleration of subordination and servitude to men. The primary sites of this reduction are the sites of heterosexual relation and encounter—courtship and marriage-arrangement, romance, sexual liaisons, fucking, marriage, prostitution, the normative family, incest and child sexual assault. It is on this terrain of heterosexual connection that girls and women are habituated to abuse, insult, and degradation, that girls are reduced to women— to wives, to whores, to mistresses, to sex slaves, to clerical workers and textile workers, to the mothers of men's children. The secondary sites of the forced female embodiment of subordination are the sites of the ritual preparations of girls and women for heterosexual intercourse, relations, or attachments. I refer to training in proper deportment and attire and decoration, all of which is training in and habituation to bodily restriction and distortion; I refer to diets and exercise and beauty regimens which habituate the individual to deprivation and punishment and to fear and suspicion of her body and its wisdom; I refer to the abduction and seasoning of female sexual slaves; to clitoridectomy and other forms and sorts of physical and spiritual mutilation; all of which have no cultural or economic purpose or function if girls and women do not have to be made ready for husbands and male lovers, pimps, johns, bosses and slavers.

Without (hetero)sexual abuse, (hetero)sexual harassment and the (hetero)sexualization of every aspect of females bodies and behaviors, there would not be patriarchy, and whatever other forms or materializations of oppression might exist, they would not have the shapes, boundaries and dynamics of the racism, nationalism, and so on that we are now familiar with.

The meanings of female heterosexuality are many, and it does not play the same political role in all social and cultural locales. But in most locales it glues each adult woman to one or more men of her caste, class, race, nation, or tribe, making her, willy nilly, a supporter of whatever politic those men adhere to, though she has little or no part in shaping or defining that politic, regardless of whether that politic is liberatory or oppressive, and regardless of whether it is liberatory for women. In the particular cases of races and classes which are politically dominant in their locale, female heterosexuality joins females in racial and/or class solidarity to dominating males and offers for their compliance the bribe of a share of the benefits their men extort from other groups. Female heterosexuality, whether literally *sexual* or not, is profoundly implicated in the racism of white women in our present time and place; the disloyalty to the civilization of white men which Adrienne Rich recommended to white women is not possible without disloyalty to the men with whom one is bonded by the institution of heterosexuality.[5] And in racial or ethnic groups which are oppressed, when a woman is not complying with the norms of female heterosexuality to the satisfaction of some man, he may bully her into line with the argument that her noncompliance or rebellion against the norms of femininity is disloyalty to her race or her community.

Lesbian feminists have noted that if the institution of female heterosexuality is what makes girls into women and is central to the continuous replication of patriarchy, then women's abandonment of that institution recommends itself as one strategy (among others) in the project of dismantling patriarchal structures. And if heterosexual encounters, relations and connections are the sites of the inscription of the patriarchal imperatives on the bodies of women, it makes sense to abandon those sites. And if female heterosexuality is central to the way sexism and racism are knit together in strange paradoxical symbiosis, it makes sense that non-participation in that institution could be part of a strategy for weakening both racism and patriarchy.

Some women speaking in other-than-lesbian feminist voices have responded by saying that withdrawal from participation in the institution of female heterosexuality is only a personal solution and only available to a few; they have said it is not a political, not a systemic strategy. I think, on the contrary, that it can be a systemic strategy, because female heterosexuality is not a given in nature, but is actively and continuously constructed. If women take the construction of ourselves and the institutions and practices which determine and govern us into our own hands, we can construct something else.

Commitment to the naturalness or inevitability of female heterosexuality is commitment to the power relations which are expressed and maintained by the institutions of female heterosexuality in patriarchal cultures around the world. (It is also, by postmodern lights, ahistorical and essentialist.) People who have power maintain that power partly by using that power to make its own historical conditions ahistorical—that is they make the prerequisites of their power into "givens." They naturalize them. A vital part of making generalized male dominance as close to inevitable as a human construction can be is the naturalization of female heterosexuality. Men have been creating ideologies and political practices which naturalize female heterosexuality continuously in every culture since the dawns of the patriarchies. (Both Freud and Lacan are naturalizers of female heterosexuality. They say that female heterosexuality is constructed, but they rescue themselves by going on to say that its construction is determined and made inevitable by the nature of civilization, or the nature of language.)

Female heterosexuality is not a biological drive or an individual woman's erotic attraction or attachment to another human animal which happens to be male. Female heterosexuality is a set of social institutions and practices defined and regulated by patriarchal kinship systems, by both civil and religious law, and by strenuously enforced mores and deeply entrenched values and taboos. Those definitions, regulations, values and taboos are about male fraternity and the oppression and exploitation of women. They are not about love, human warmth, solace, fun, pleasure, or deep knowledge between people. If any of the latter arise within the boundaries of these institutions and practices, it is because fun, solace, pleasure and acknowledgement grow like dandelions and are hard to eradicate, not because heterosexuality is natural or is naturally a site of such benefits.

So, is it possible to be a feminist without being a lesbian? My inclination is to say that feminism, which is thoroughly antipatriarchal, is not compatible with female heterosexuality, which is thoroughly patriarchal. But I anticipate the following reply:

"You seem to suppose that all relation, connection, or encounter of any passionate or erotic or genital sort or involving any sort of personal commitment between a female and a male must belong to this patriarchal institution called "female heterosexuality," that it must be suffocated by this rubric,...you seem therefore to suppose that our acts and feelings and meanings are all totally formed by history, social institutions and language. That is a kind of hopeless determinism which is politically fatal and is contradicted by your own presence here as a lesbian."

I agree that I cannot embrace any absolute historical, social determinism. The feminist lesbians' permanent project of defining ourselves and our passions and our communities is a living willful refusal of such determinism. But the free space of creation exists only when it is actively, creatively, aggressively, courageously, persistently occupied. Patriarchal histories and cultures mitigate against such space constantly, by material and conceptual coercion, by bribery, by punishment and by shaping and constraining the imagination. So long as we do not actively, perversely and obstinately create ourselves, lesbians are impossible.

In my essay "To Be And Be Seen," following up on a tip from Sarah Hoagland, I explored at length the proposition that there are no lesbians in the universes of patriarchy. A similar and more generic point is useful here.

The word "virgin" did not originally mean a woman whose vagina was untouched by any penis, but a free woman, one not betrothed, not married, not bound to, not possessed by any man. It meant a female who is sexually and hence socially her own person. In any universe of patriarchy, there are no Virgins in this sense. Even female children are possessed by their male kin and are conceived of as potential wives. Hence Virgins must be unspeakable, thinkable only as negations, their existence impossible. Radically feminist lesbians have claimed positive Virginity and have been inventing ways of living it out, in creative defiance of patriarchal definitions of the real, the meaningful. The question at hand may be conceived this way: *Will* and *can* any women, many women, creatively defy patriarchal definitions of the real and the meaningful to invent and embody modes of living positive Virginity which include women's maintaining erotic, economic, home-making, partnering connections with men? Such Virgins are no more possible *in* patriarchy than are lesbians, and if they impossibly bring themselves into existence, they will be living lives as sexually, socially and politically outlandish and unnatural as the lives undertaken by radically feminist lesbians. What must be imagined here is females who are willing to engage in chosen connections with males, who are wild, undomesticated females, creating themselves here and now.

In a way, it is not my place to imagine these wild females who have occasional and/or committed erotic, reproductive, home-making, partnered or friendship relations with males. The work and the pleasure of that imagining belong to those who undertake to invent themselves thus. But I do have a vivid, though partial, image of them. It derives both from my own experience as an impossible being and from my intense desire for alliance and sisterhood with women of my acquaintance who engage in relations with men in the patriarchal context but who also seem to me to have a certain aptitude for Virginity. This image expresses that "perverse optimism" which I said at the beginning is one source of this writing/speaking. So I offer for your consideration a sketch of my image of these wild women: (This is not a recipe for political correctness, and I am not legislating: this is a report from my Imagination.)

These Virgins do not attire and decorate themselves in the gear which in their cultures signal female compliance with male-defined femininity and which would form their bodies to such compliance. They do not make themselves "attractive" in the conventional feminine modes of their cultures and so people who can ignore their animal beauty say they are ugly. They maintain as much economic flexibility as they possibly can to ensure that they can revert to independence any time economic partnership is binding them to an alliance less than fully chosen. They would no more have sex when they don't expect to enjoy it than they would run naked in the rain when they don't expect to enjoy it. Their sexual interactions are not sites where people with penises make themselves men and people with vaginas are made women.[6]

These Virgins who connect with men don't try to maintain the fictions that the men they favor are better men than other men. When they are threatened by people who feel threatened by them, they do not point to their connections with men as soothing proof that they really aren't manhaters. They don't avail themselves of male protection. They do not pressure their daughters or their mothers, sisters, friends or students to relate to men in the ways they do so they can feel validated by the other women's choices. They never consider bringing any man with them to any feminist gathering that is not specifically meant to include men, and they help to create and to defend (and they enjoy) women-only spaces.

These Virgins who connect with men are not manipulable by orchestrations of male approval and disapproval, orchestrations of men's and children's needs, real or fake. They are not capable of being reduced to conformity by dread or anxiety about things lesbian, and are unafraid of their own passions for other Virgins, including those who are lesbians. They do not need to be respectable.

These Virgins refuse to enter the institution of marriage, and do not support or witness the weddings of others, including the weddings of their favorite brothers. They are die-hard marriage-resisters. They come under enormous pressure to marry, but they do not give in to it. They do not consider marriage a privilege. Not even the bribe of spousal health insurance benefits lures them into marriage, not even as they and their partners get older and become more anxious about their health and their economic situations.

These Virgins have strong, reliable, creative, enduring, sustaining, ardent friendships with women. Their imagination and their politics are shaped more fundamentally by a desire to empower women and create friendship and solidarity among women than by a commitment to appease, comfort or change men. These Virgins who connect with men do not feel that they could be themselves and be in closets; they are "out" as loose and noncompliant females, a very noticeable phenomenon on the social and political scene. They make themselves visible, audible and tangible to each other, they make community and sisterhood with each other and with lesbian Virgins, and they support each other in their wildness. They frolic and make trouble together. They create ways to have homes and warmth and companionship and intensity with or without a man included. They create value and they create meaning, so when the pressures to conform to patriarchal female heterosexuality are great, they have a context and community of resistance to sustain them and to engage their creative energies in devising new solutions to the problems conformity pretends to solve.

They create music, novels, poetry, art, magazines and newspapers, knowledge, skills and tools, political actions and programs. And in their magazines and newspapers, they articulate their imagination, their cultural and political differences, their various values; they berate each other, they support each other, they pay attention to each other.

A re these beings I imagine possible? Can you fuck without losing your virginity? I think everything is against it, but *it's not my call*. I can hopefully image, but the counter-possible creation of such a reality is up to those who want to live it, if anyone does.

S ome women have hoped that you *do* have to be a lesbian to be a real, extreme, to-the-root, troublemaking feminist, because then, since they are not lesbians and would never in the world become lesbians, they have an excuse for not thinking or acting radically feminist and not alienating men. Much of what passes for women's fear of lesbianism is really fear of men—fear of what men might do to non-compliant females. But I do not want to provide such an excuse for moderate or safe feminism.

"Do you have to be a lesbian to be a feminist?" is not quite the right question. The question should be "Can a woman be heterosexual and be radically feminist?" My picture is this: you do not have to be a lesbian to uncompromisingly embody and enact a radical feminism, but you also cannot be heterosexual in any standard patriarchal meaning of that word—you cannot be any version of a patriarchal wife. Lesbian or not, to embody and enact a consistent and all-the-way feminism you have to be a heretic, a deviant, an undomesticated female, an impossible being. You have to be a Virgin.

---

[1] This is a slightly revised version of a speech I gave, titled "Do You Have To Be A Lesbian To Be A Feminist?", at the National Women's Studies Association annual conference in June, 1990, in Akron Ohio. I was invited to be one of two speakers in a plenary session which I was told would be on lesbianism, feminism, and homophobia, though when the program came out, there was another title given to the session, a title which did not include the word 'lesbian'. The original speech was published in *off our backs* in the August/September issue, 1990, and sparked a flood of very critical letters to the editor from women who thought I had answered the title question "yes."

I am happy to acknowledge Carolyn Shafer's help in thinking through and crafting these reflections, and I am indebted also to discussion with Maria Lugones which helped me have the courage to cut through some confusions.

[2] In some cultural contexts, this intimacy would not be considered *sexual*. Indeed, in my own time and place, it is difficult for some people to think of intimacy between women as really "sexual." Cf. Frye, "To Be And Be Seen," in *The Politics of Reality: Essays in Feminist Theory* (Freedom, California: The Crossing Press, 1983) 156-158.

[3] In the context of European and North American cultures, it may have been a mark of women's increased status (a result of the successes of the 19th Century feminism) that intimate relations among women have come to be taken seriously enough by patriarchal authorities to be seen as an extension of the sexual and to be rigidly forbidden.

[4] Thanks to Miriam Johnson for encouraging me to be more mindful, here, of the cultural specificity of the concepts of 'lesbian' and 'heterosexual'. She suggested that the term 'wife' more accurately designates what women are required to be, cross-culturally, than the term 'heterosexual'. But in the middle-class U.S. culture of which I am a native, at this time the legal and traditional meaning of 'wife' is too narrow to designate what I am referring to. Women of my culture are not so strenuously required to marry as they are required to be heterosexual—to be sexually available to a man or men and not to "be sexual with" women.

[5] "Disloyal to Civilization: Feminism, Racism, and Gynephobia," *On Lies, Secrets, and Silence* (NY: Norton, 1979) 275-310. See also "White Woman Feminist" in this collection.

[6] These felicitous phrases are due to John Stoltenberg, *Refusing To Be A Man: Essays on Sex and Justice* (Portland, Oregon: Breitenbush Books, Inc.) *passim*.

A Response to <u>Lesbian Ethics:</u> Why Ethics?[1]

In conjunction with the publication of her book *Lesbian Ethics*,[2] Sarah Hoagland gave a number of talks to lesbian community audiences around the country. At one point, I was called upon to do the introduction at one of these talks. In my introduction, I said, "We are hungry for ethics—we crave moral clarity." This line was well-received by the audience it was written for; it seemed to speak the feelings of many of those present. I proceeded, saying that patriarchal fathers feed that hunger with an ethics of rules which works like junk-food—temporarily and deceptively soothing the longing without meeting the need. Enjoying my metaphor, I went on to say that what *Lesbian Ethics* offered was the equivalent of delicious bran muffins. Her book is indeed tasty and expeditious food for thought. But in suggesting that it provides an ethics which meets our need for an ethics, I was very much oversimplifying...indeed, I now think, falsifying, both our need and what this book might accomplish.

I spoke of a hunger for ethics. Why the hunger and whose hunger is it? I was speaking of something I recognized in myself and in many of the women in my lesbian community. The first thing that comes to mind to explain why such women are hungry for ethics is that both as feminists and as lesbians, we have in significant ways and degrees rejected and abandoned the values we grew up with and many of the central values of the cultures in which, willy nilly, we live and work, and we are trying now to make decisions, choices and judgments pretty much without the guidance of a system of values we can accept and endorse. We fall back, of course, as Sarah Hoagland has pointed out, into habits of action and interaction which express the values of patriarchy but we are very displeased when we realize we have done that. We want a new, and different ethics to fill the void, so we will have a positive alternative and can know what to do and have some confidence, when we have acted, that we have done right.

But this does not answer my question. I'm wondering about the need to know what to do and have confidence that we have acted rightly. Not why we feel we need a *new* ethics, but why we need an ethics at all. I'm wondering if that need itself isn't something that could be given up, indeed, if I dare say so, perhaps *should* be given up.

My intuition is that the need for an ethics is race, class and history specific, that ethics is a practice and institution that would arise only among people occupying certain positions in certain social orders. That is too grand a theory to argue for here. But at least one sort of need for an ethics is characteristic only of people with an investment of a certain sort in being good and/or in others' being good, in doing the right thing, being right or being in the right. Not everyone at every time has such an investment. I will briefly discuss here two sorts of reasons why women like myself—white, christian-cultured and educated, in our times, in the U.S.—would tend to have a need for an ethics. Both of these reasons are such that exploring them suggests it would be a good idea not to try to satisfy the need but to try to grow out of it.

In an earlier paper of mine, I articulated such a need quite dramatically. It was in the context of a crisis in my effort to respond constructively to criticism of myself and my work as racist. I had come to realize that not only my acts but my capacities for self-criticism and correction were contaminated by racism, and that therefore there seemed to be no way to fix what was wrong with me. I wrote:

> It all combined to precipitate me into profound and unnerving distrust of myself. All of my ways of knowing seemed to have failed me—my perception, my common sense, my good will, my anger, honor and affection, my intelligence and insight. Just as walking requires something fairly sturdy and firm underfoot, so being an actor in the world requires a foundation of ordinary moral and intellectual confidence. Without that, we don't know how

to be or how to act; we become strangely stupid... If you want to be good, and you don't know good from bad, you can't move.[3]

The phrase that strikes me, and even when I wrote it stood out as peculiar, is the phrase "don't know how to be or how to act." It suggests that before these developments in my personal and political life, I knew how to be and how to act. How, one might wonder, did I know to be, and know to act? And on what had I based my "ordinary moral confidence"?

A description of what might be thought of as being taught moral confidence was given by Minnie Bruce Pratt in her essay in the volume *Yours, In Struggle*. Describing the orientation to matters of right and wrong with which she had been raised, she says: "I was taught to be a *judge*, of moral responsibility and of punishment only in relation to *my* ethical system; was taught to be a *martyr*, to take all responsibility for change, *and* the glory, to expect others to do nothing; was taught to be a *peacemaker*, to mediate, negotiate, between opposing sides because *I* knew the right way; was taught to be a *preacher*, to point out wrongs and tell others what to do."[4]

I was taught something like this, growing up in a small town south of the Mason-Dixon line, in an upwardly mobile and self-consciously christian and white family. I learned that I, and "we" knew right from wrong and had the responsibility to see to it right was done; that there were others, who did not know what is right and wrong and should be advised, instructed, helped and directed by us. What I was being taught, in effect, as Carolyn Shafer put it in conversation, was that Right makes Might. Not that Might makes Right. The other way around. I was being taught that *because* one knows what is right, it is morally appropriate to have and exercise what I now would call race privilege and class privilege...to dominate others. Only we did not think of it as "dominating." Knowing right from wrong is what constitutes one as a certain sort of agent in the world. One *understands* one's agency *as* that of the judge, teacher/preacher, director, administrator, manager, and in this mode, as a decision maker, planner, policy maker, organizer. Such a one knows how to be and how to act. Such a person trusts its moral sensibilities.

This is clearly a cultural context in which individuals would have a vital investment in knowing what is right and wrong, in being right, in being in the right. Knowing this is constitutive of the kind of agency they understand and animate.

If one is not simply white/christian/middle-class/"American," but also a woman, there is a nasty twist in the middle of this pretty picture. Judging, preaching, directing, administering, managing, policy making are not feminine vocations. This sort of agency is male, in the scheme of the upright, educated, christian gentry. The women of this group have, perhaps since sometime in the last century, tended to divide up into those who accept the feminine parallel vocation of motherhood and community service and those who are ambitious for the "full personhood" held by the males of that social-racial group. The latter may become either Athenas or feminists. If one gets a certain sort of male sponsorship, becomes a Daddy's girl, one is allowed to function in these vocations of the righteous, so long, that is, as one is doing things one's sponsors approve of. One's rightness is not really one's own, in this case, but is one's sponsors' rightness. One's authority is effective only so long as one identifies wholly with the sponsors.[5] What happens for the feminist is that she somehow discovers her *own* authority, and comes to understand herself as authorized by her *own* knowledge of right and wrong to assume the agency of the judge, director, instructor, planner, policy maker, administrator.

This feminist—white, christian-cultured, educated, born or assimilated to the middle class—is someone with a doubly determined investment in knowing what is right and wrong. Her knowledge of right and wrong is constitutive of how she conceives her agency and that it is her *own* knowledge is the key to her conceiving her agency *as her own.*

Well, no wonder she is completely demoralized and petrified by the discovery that she does not, after all, know right from wrong. And no wonder this woman hungers for ethics. She craves clarity and confidence about what are the right ways to act and to be with the whole energy of her passion for Be-ing, for Presence, for Ability, for Agency.

But only people situated just so in culture, economy and history ground their understanding of their agency in being right, righteous and in the right: namely, those people who must have a foundation for assuming the direction and administration of everything. And Lesbian Nation does not need a class of citizens whose vocation is to run it. And if we can do without such a class of citizens and thus without such a conception of agency, we will not have this ground of a need for ethics, at least not this need.

Returning to the quotation I drew from my earlier work coping with the discovery of my racism, there is another phrase in it that directs us to another source of the need for ethics. I said, "If you want to be good, and you don't know good from bad, you can't move." At that time, in that context, I very much wanted to be good. I wanted to view myself as good, and to be perceived as good; but I also simply wanted to *be* good.

Why should one want to be good? Why, in particular, would a woman want to be good?

We may recall some of the message of Mary Daly's *Gyn/Ecology.*[6] A great deal of the machinery of men's oppression and exploitation of women consists of mechanisms by which women's own energies and resources are turned against us, to suppress our spirits, cloud our judgment and consume us. And one of the most effective devices for this is the construction and manipulation of good and evil. It is a complex strategy. One part is the identification of certain things as good and others as evil—the naming of vices and virtues, and of sins. These are falsely and deceptively named. Almost anything that would strengthen or empower us or inspire us with the spirit of rebellion will be named "evil" or "sinful." But this is not enough. We may not avoid the things called "evil," especially since our animal wisdom would generally move us toward them. We must be motivated to heed this naming.

What's needed is *both* the naming of certain things as "good" and "evil" *and* women's wanting the "good" and shunning the "evil." Ideally, we should be gotten to care enormously for the "good" and strenuously to dread the "evil." This is accomplished by naming *women* "evil." Eve, Pandora, The Witch, The Stepmother, The Mother-in-law, the Whore etc. Naming women "evil" makes it open season on women—to be "punished," used, scapegoated, ignored, abused. This gives us motivation to attempt to dissociate ourselves from "evil" and associate ourselves with "good." Hence, we are drawn into the contradictory and self-defeating project of trying to distance ourselves from the category of *woman* by constantly demonstrating, by being good, that we are "exceptional women." Since *woman* is by definition evil, this project can never be once-and-for-all completed, and we are bound up in it for life, that is, bound up for life in proving that there is nothing of Eve, Pandora, the Witch, the Stepmother, the Mother-in-Law or the Whore in us, i.e., nothing of independence, autonomy or rebellion. Women are, then, locked in to a project of being good which is fundamentally defensive and intrinsically Self-defeating, and which establishes an urgent need for an ethics to tell us how to be good.

But now I want to modify this picture of woman in patriarchy with another intuition about the race, class and historical *specificity* of it. This is suggested to me by many things, but most recently by Vicki Spelman's discussion of Aristotle in her new book, *Inessential Woman.*[7] As I read it, she is saying that everything Aristotle says about women is about, not female human beings, but the wives and potential wives of citizens; in Aristotle, "men and women" means "citizens and their wives." Females slaves and foreigners, and wives of artisans and merchants are not "women." Only humans of a certain class have gender. I suspect that the whole scenario Daly uncovered, of the oppressive manipulation of "good" and "evil" and the manipulation of women through it, is a scenario developed by "citizens" for the construction and reduction of their women, and only spills over in some ways and at some times into the structures that shape the lives of women and men who do not have the status of "citizens." And it seems to me that when a woman (a female with certain kinship relations to members of the citizen class) is "bad" or "evil" she is *not* a "citizen," and is reduced to being a mere female.[8] Being "good" is required to retain her precarious status of "citizen-ess"—a status which by birth she gets a crack at.

In the subculture I grew up in, this distinction between citizenesses and other females was marked semantically by the distinction between 'woman' and 'lady'. As daughters of citizens our mission was to distinguish ourselves from women (who were "bad") and construct ourselves as ladies (who were "good"). Those young women of this subculture who had serious intellectual, political, or economic ambitions recognized that we had to repudiate ladyhood, and we reverted to trying to convince the world (men) that women could be good and hence could deserve or earn the rights, privileges, and safety granted to (male) citizens as a birthright. This is still the project of much of feminist ethics and of much of the lesbian civil rights movement.

Females of many other subcultures in this society (and of many other cultures elsewhere) have no chance of becoming citizenesses, and correspondingly, no such structured-in urgency about being good. I suspect that women who passionately desire to be good are most often women who can suppose that by being good they can achieve vicarious citizenship, that is, vicarious participation in the privileges and privileged status of the dominating races and classes. Women with no such hope would not be likely to manifest their ambition for dignity, soundness of character and judgment, and effectiveness in the world, as a desire to be good.

If this is so, it seems like it would behoove women who claim to abhor race and class privilege to give up the habit of pursuing them by being and trying to be good. The discovery that one is not good, or doesn't know how to be good, might be welcomed as releasing one from the game of "good" and "evil" and thus from the will-bindings that keep us bonded to our oppressors.

I am seeing the need for ethics in lesbian and feminist communities where I reside, understood as a need to know right from wrong, know the good, act right and be good, as a need particular to women trying to earn or maintain a certain kind of status. In my own experience, it seems to me that this is a quite distinctive kind of preoccupation with ethics and that it is more prevalent among white, middle-class raised or assimilated, christian-cultured women than among women rooted in other cultural matrices.[9] Thinking on this leads me to wonder if instead of seeking to create a Lesbian Ethics, many of us who are attracted by a book titled *Lesbian Ethics* might consider learning to do without ethics entirely.

And I think that it may turn out that this is what Sarah Hoagland's book will help us accomplish.

She is shifting from the language of the modern tradition of ethics: from knowing what is right or good to deciding what to pay attention to. And her last section is about *meaning*, the creation of meaning, not about "ethics." This book will *not* meet the need for an ethics which may motivate many of those who purchase it. It is, in fact, quite a frustrating book so long as one clings to that need.

Hoagland's central thesis is that agency can be understood as the creation and maintenance of meaning and value, and what she offers as "ethics" is an open-ended exploration of what kinds of actions and strategies in various situations (and in particular in situations of oppression) have created or might create what meanings and values. It is somewhat "empirical," as in some degree it is a matter of learning and recording what dynamics of interpretation and interaction do arise from the pursuit of certain strategies in certain situations; it is in part a creative project generating novel dynamics of interpretation and interaction through novel acts and strategies. Such an "ethics" makes no pretense at all of telling us what is right or how to be good, but I think it can, if it is allowed to, seduce those of us who feel we need such things into a new space much further from our citizen fathers' homes, where "right" and "good" no longer trick us into continuing our dutiful-daughterhoods.

¹ This is a slightly revised version of a talk composed for a panel on Hoagland's *Lesbian Ethics* at the meeting of the Midwest Division of the Society for Women in Philosophy, March 19, 1989, in Indianapolis, which was published as "A Response to *Lesbian Ethics*," HYPATIA 5, no.3(Fall 1990), pp.132-137. It was reprinted in *Feminist Ethics*, edited by Claudia Card (Lawrence, Kansas: University Press of Kansas, 1991). My thanks to Claudia Card for suggestions which helped me make various points clearer and more accurate.

² Hoagland, Sarah Lucia, *Lesbian Ethics: Toward New Value* (Palo Alto, CA: Institute of Lesbian Studies, 1988).

³ See "White Woman Feminist" in this volume. Much of the material in the next three paragraphs is drawn from that essay. That essay and this one locate those same observations on two different axes of exploration.

⁴ "Identity: Skin Blood Heart," *Yours in Struggle: Three Feminist Perspectives on Anti-Semitism and Racism*, edited by Elly Bulkin, Minnie Bruce Pratt and Barbara Smith (Brooklyn, NY: Long Haul Press, 1984).

⁵ For a useful discussion of the nuclear family dynamics associated with this "Athena," see: Miriam M. Johnson, *Strong Mothers, Weak Wives* (Berkeley: University of California Press, 1988).

⁶ Daly, Mary, *Gyn/Ecology: The Metaethics of Radical Feminism* (Boston: Beacon Press, 1984).

⁷ Spelman, Elizabeth V., *Inessential Woman: Problems of Exclusion in Feminist Thought* (Boston: Beacon Press, 1989), pp. 45-47.

⁸ In contemporary U.S. circumstances, women who are divorced gener-

ally suffer a radical reduction in their standard of living, often ending up "on welfare," which is a contemporary equivalent of having lost the status of "citizen." Good women, of course, keep their husbands and do not cause their children to live in poverty.

[9] I am not suggesting that women of other racial, ethnic and religious cultures and traditions do not care about ethics. Many cultures and traditions place great emphasis on ethics (conceived in a variety of ways) and women of these cultures and traditions clearly care immensely about justice, about doing right by others, about dignity and responsibility and about being decent human beings. I am talking here about a particular kind of need for ethics and a particular understanding of ethics that is tailored to that need. It seems to me that having that sort of interest in ethics *reduces* a woman's working capacity for a more-than-rhetorical commitment to justice, dignity and responsibility.

White Woman Feminist
1983-1992

Introduction

This essay is the latest version of something I have been re-writing ever since my essay "On Being White" was published in *The Politics of Reality*. In a way, this *is* that first essay, emerging after several metamorphoses.

"On Being White" grew out of experiences I had in my home lesbian community in which I was discovering some of what it means for a woman, a feminist, to be white. These were very frustrating experiences: they played out and revealed the ways in which the fact that I am white gave unbidden and unwanted meanings to my thought and my actions and poisoned them all with privilege.

An intermediate version of this work, delivered at various colleges and universities around 1984-86, began with the following account of my attempts to come to grips with the fact of being white in a white-supremacist racist state, and with some of the criticism my first effort had drawn.[1]

> Many white feminists, myself included, have tried to identify and change the attitudes and behaviors which blocked our friendly and effective comradeship with women of color and limited our ability to act against institutional racism. I assumed at first that these revisions would begin with analysis and decision: I had to understand the problems and then do whatever would effect the changes dictated by this understanding. But as I entered this work, I almost immediately learned that my competence to do it was questionable.

The idea was put to me by several women of color (and was stated in writings by women of color) that a white woman is not in a good position to analyze institutional or personal racism and a white woman's decisions about what to do about racism cannot be authentic. About conscious-raising groups for white women, Sharon Keller said to me in a letter, "I think that there are things which white women working together can accomplish but I do not think that white women are in the best positions usually to know what those things are or when it is the right time to do them. It would go a long way...for white women to take seriously their [relative] helplessness in this matter." White women's analysis of their own racism has also often been heard by women of color as "mere psychologizing."...To be rid of racism, a white woman may indeed have to do some intro-specting, remembering and verbalizing of feelings, but the self-knowledge which she might achieve by this work would necessarily produce profound change, and there are many reasons why many white women may not want to change. White women's efforts to gain self-knowledge are easily undermined by the desire not to live out the consequences of getting it; their/our projects of consciousness-raising and self-analysis are very susceptible to the slide from "working on yourself" to "playing with yourself."...Apparently the white woman herself is ill-situated for telling which is which...

All of my ways of knowing seemed to have failed me— my perception, my common sense, my good will, my anger, honor and affection, my intelligence and insight. Just as walking requires something fairly sturdy and firm underfoot, so being an actor in the world requires a foundation of ordinary moral and intellectual confidence. Without that, we don't know how to be or how to act; we become strangely stupid; the commitment against racism becomes itself immo-bilizing. Even obvious and easy acts either do not occur to us or threaten to be racist by presumptuous assumptions or misjudged timing, wording, or circumstances. Simple things like courtesy or giving money, attending a trial, working on a project initiated by women of color, or dissenting from racist views expressed in white company become fraught with possibilities of error and offense. If you want to do good, and you don't know good from bad, you can't move.[2] Thus stranded, we also learned that it was exploitive and oppres-sive to ask for the help of women of color in extricating ourselves from this ignorance, confusion, incompetence and moral failure. Our racism is our problem, not theirs.[3]

Some white women report that the great enemy of their efforts to combat their own racism is their feelings of guilt. That is not my own experience, or that is not my word for it. The great enemies in my heart have been the despair and the resentment which come with being required (by others and by my own integrity) to repair something apparently irreparable, required to take responsibility for something apparently beyond my powers to effect. Both confounded and angry, my own temptation is to collapse—to admit defeat and retire from the field. What counteracts that temptation, for me, seems to be little more than willfulness and lust: I *will* not be broken, and my appetite for woman's touch is not, thank goodness, thoroughly civilized to the established categories. But if I cannot give up and I cannot act, what do Will and Lust recommend? The obvious way out of the relentless logic of my situation is to cease being white.

The Contingency of Racedness

I was brought up with a concept of race according to which you cannot stop being the race you are: your race is an irreversible physical, indeed, ontological fact about you. But when the criteria for membership in a race came up as an issue among white people I knew, considerations of skin color and biological lineage were not definitive or decisive, or rather, they were so precisely when white people decided they should be, and were not when white people wanted them not to be. As I argued in "On Being White",[4] white people actively legislate matters of race membership, and if asserting their right to do so requires making decisions that override physical criteria, they ignore physical criteria (without, of course, ever abandoning the ideological strategy of insisting the categories are given in nature). This sort of behavior clearly demonstrates that people construct race, actively, and that people who think they are unquestionably white generally think the criteria of what it is to be of this race or that are theirs to manipulate.[5]

Being white is not a biological condition. It is being a member of a certain social/political category, a category that is persistently maintained by those people who are, in their own and each others' perception, most unquestionably in it. It is like being a member of a political party, or a club, or a fraternity—or being a Methodist or a Mormon. If one is white one is a member of a continuously and politically constituted group which holds itself together by rituals of unity and exclusion, which develops in its members certain styles and attitudes useful in the exploitation of others, which demands and rewards fraternal loyalty, which defines itself as the paradigm of humanity, and which rationalizes (and naturalizes) its existence and its practices of exclusion, colonization, slavery and genocide (when it bothers to) in terms of a mythology of blood and skin. If you were born to people who are members of that club, you are socialized and inducted into that club. Your membership in it is in a way, or to a degree, compulsory—nobody gave you any choice in the matter—but it is contingent and, in the Aristotelian sense, accidental. Well then, if you don't like being a member of that club, you might think of resigning your membership, or of figuring out how to get yourself kicked out of the club, how to get yourself excommunicated.

But this strategy of "separation" is vulnerable to a variety of criticisms. A white woman cannot cease having the history she has by some sort of divorce ritual. Furthermore, the renunciation of whiteness may be an act of self-loathing rather than an act of liberation.[6] And disassociation from the race-group one was born into might seem to be an option for white folks, but seems either not possible or not politically desirable to most members of the other groups from which the whites set themselves off.[7] This criticism suggests that my thinking of disassociating from membership in the white fraternity is just another exercise (hence, another reinforcement) of that white privilege which I was finding so onerous and attempting to escape. All these criticisms sound right (and I will circle back to them at the end of the essay), but there is something very wrong here. This closure has the distinctive finality of a trap.

In academic circles where I now circulate, it has become a commonplace that race is a "social construction" and not a naturally given and naturally maintained grouping of human individuals with naturally determined sets of traits. And the recognition of race as non-natural is presumed, in those circles, to be liberatory. Pursuing the idea of disassociating from the race-category in which I am placed and from the perquisites attached to it is a way of pursuing the question of what freedom can be made of this, and for whom. But it is seeming to me that race (together with racism and race privilege) is apparently *constructed as* something inescapable. And it makes sense that it would be, since such a construction would best serve those served by race and racism. *Of course* race and racism are impossible to escape; of course a white person is always in a sticky web of privilege that permits only acts which reinforce ("reinscribe") racism. This just means that some exit must be forced. That will require conceptual creativity, and perhaps conceptual violence.

The "being white" that has presented itself to me as a burden and an insuperable block to my growth out of racism is not essentially about the color of my skin or any other inherited bodily trait, even though doctrines of color are bound up with this status in some ways. The problem then, is to find a way to think clearly about some kind of whiteness that is *not essentially* tied to color and yet has some significant relation to color. The distinction feminists have made between maleness and masculinity provides a clue and an analogy. Maleness we have construed as something a human animal can be born with; masculinity we have construed as something a human animal can be trained to—and it is an empirical fact that most male human animals are trained to it in one or another of its cultural varieties.[8] Masculinity is not a blossoming consequence of genetic constitution as lush growths of facial hair seem to be in the males of many human groups. But the masculinity of an adult male is far from superficial or incidental and we know it is not something an individual could shrug off like a coat or snap out of like an actor stepping out of his character. The masculinity of an adult male human in any particular culture is also profoundly connected with the local perceptions and conceptions of maleness (as "biological"), its causes and its consequences. So it may be with being white, but we need some revision of our vocabulary to say it rightly. We need a term in the realm of race and racism whose grammar is analogous to the grammar of the term 'masculinity'. I am tempted to recommend the neologism 'albosity' for this honor, but I'm afraid it is too strange to catch on. So I will introduce 'whitely' and 'whiteliness' as terms whose grammar is analogous to that of 'masculine' and 'masculinity'. Being white-skinned (like being male) is a matter of physical traits presumed to be physically determined; being whitely (like being masculine) I conceive as a deeply ingrained way of being in the world. Following the analogy with masculinity, I assume that the connection between whiteliness and light-colored skin is a *contingent* connection: this character could be manifested by persons who are *not* "white;" it can be absent in persons who *are*.

In the next section, I will talk about whiteliness in a free and speculative way, exploring what it may be. This work is raw preliminary sketching; it moves against no such background of research and attentive observation as there is to guide accounts of masculinity. There is of course a large literature on racism, but I think that what I am after here is not one and the same thing as racism, either institutional or personal. Whiteliness is connected to institutional racism (as will emerge further on in the discussion) by the fact that individuals with this sort of character are well-suited to the social roles of agents of institutional racism, but it is a character of persons, not of institutions. Whiteliness is also related to individual or personal racism, but I think it is not one and the same thing as racism, at least in the sense where 'racism' means bigotry/hate/ignorance/indifference. As I understand masculinity it is not the same thing as misogyny; similarly, whiteliness is not the same thing as race-hatred. One can be whitely even if one's beliefs and feelings are relatively well-informed, humane and good-willed. So I approach whiteliness freshly, as itself, as something which is both familiar and unknown.

Whiteliness

To begin to get a picture of what whiteliness is, we need to invoke a certain candid and thoughtful reflection on the part of white people, who of course in some ways know themselves best; we also need to listen to what people of color perceive of white people, since in some ways they know white people best. For purposes of this brief and preliminary exploration, I will draw on material from three books for documentation of how white people are as presented in the experience of people of color. The three are *This Bridge Called My Back*,[9] which is a collection of writings by radical women of color, *Feminist Theory: From Margin to Center*,[10] by Black theorist bell hooks, and *Drylongso*,[11] which is a collection of narratives of members of what its editor calls the "core black community."[12] For white voices, I draw on my own and on those I have heard as a participant/observer of white culture, and on Minnie Bruce Pratt.

Minnie Bruce Pratt, a feminist and a white southerner, has spelled out some of what I would call the whitely way of dealing with issues of morality and change.[13] She said she had been taught to be a *judge*—a judge of responsibility and of punishment, according to an ethical system which countenances no rival; she had been taught to be a *preacher*—to point out wrongs and tell others what to do; she had been taught to be a *martyr*—to take all responsibility and all glory; she had been taught to be a *peacemaker*—because she could see all sides and see how it all ought to be. I too was taught something like this, growing up in a small town south of the Mason-Dixon line, in a self-consciously christian and white family. I learned that I, and "we," knew right from wrong and had the responsibility to see to it right was done; that there were others who did not know what is right and wrong and should be advised, instructed, helped and directed by us. I was taught that *because* one knows what is right, it is morally appropriate to have and exercise what I now would call race privilege and class privilege. Not "might is right," but "right is might," as Carolyn Shafer put the point.[14] In any matter in which we did not know what is right, through youth or inexpertise of some sort, we would await the judgment or instruction of another (white) person who does.

> *Drylongso*: White people are bolder because they think they are supposed to know everything anyhow. (97)
>
> White men look up to their leaders more than we do and they are not much good without their leaders. (99)
>
> White people don't really know how they feel about anything until they consult their leaders or a book or other things outside themselves. (99)
>
> White people are not supposed to be stupid, so they tend to think they are intelligent, no matter how stupidly they are behaving. (96)
>
> *Margin*: The possibility [they] were not the best spokespeople for all women made [them] fear for [their] self-worth. (13)

Whitely people generally consider themselves to be benevolent and good-willed, fair, honest and ethical. The judge, preacher, peacemaker, martyr, socialist, professional, moral majority, liberal, radical, conservative, working men and women—nobody admits to being prejudiced, everybody has earned every cent they ever had, doesn't take sides, doesn't hate anybody, and always votes for the person they think best qualified for the job, regardless of the candidates' race, sex, religion or national origin, maybe even regardless of their sexual preferences. The professional version of this person is always profoundly insulted by the suggestion that s/he might have permitted some personal feeling about a client to affect the quality of services rendered. S/he believes with perfect confidence that s/he is not prejudiced, not a bigot, not spiteful, jealous or rude, does not engage in favoritism or discrimination. When there is a serious and legitimate challenge, a negotiator has to find a resolution which enables the professional person to save face, to avoid simply agreeing that s/he made an unfair or unjust judgment, discriminated against someone or otherwise behaved badly. Whitely people have a staggering faith in their own rightness and goodness, and that of other whitely people. We are not crooks.

> *Drylongso*: Every reasonable black person thinks that most white people do not mean him well. (7)
>
> They figure, if nobody blows the whistle, then nothing wrong has gone down. (21)
>
> White people are very interested in seeming to be of service...(4)
>
> Whitefolks *can't* do right, even if there was one who wanted to...They are so damn greedy and cheap that it even hurts them to *try* to do right. (59)
>
> *Bridge*: A child is trick-or-treating with her friends. At one house the woman, after realizing the child was an Indian, "quite crudely told me so, refusing to give me treats my friends had received." (47)
>
> *Drylongso*: I used to be a waitress, and I can still remember how white people would leave a tip and then someone at the table, generally some white woman, would take some of the money. (8)

Bridge: The lies, pretensions, the snobbery and cliqu-
ishness. (69)

We experience white feminists and their orga-
nizations as elitist, crudely insensitive, and
condescending. (86)

White people are so rarely loyal. (59)

Whitely people do have a sense of right and wrong, and
are ethical. Their ethics is in great part an ethics of forms,
procedures and due process. As Minnie Bruce Pratt said, their
morality is a matter of "ought-to," not "want to" or "passionately desire to." And the "oughts" tend to factor out into
propriety or good manners and abiding by the rules. Change
cannot be initiated unless the moves are made in appropriate
ways. The rules are often-rehearsed. I have participated in whitely
women's affirming to each other that some uncomfortable dis-
ruption caused by someone objecting to some injustice or offense could have been avoided: had she brought "her" problem
forth in the correct way, it could have been correctly processed.
We say:

She should have brought it up in the business meeting.

She should have just taken the other woman aside and
explained that the remark had offended her.

She should not have personally attacked me; she should
have just told me that my behavior made her uncomfortable, and I would have stopped doing it.

She should take this through the grievance procedure.

By believing in rules, by being arbiters of rules, by
understanding agency in terms of the applications of principles to particular situations, whitely people think they preserve their detachment from prejudice, bias, meanness and so
on. Whitely people tend to believe that one preserves one's
goodness by being principled, by acting according to rules instead of according to feeling.

Drylongso: We think white people are the most unprin-
cipled folks in the world... (8)

White people are some writing folks! They will write! They write everything. Now they do that because they don't trust each other. Also, they are the kind of people who think that you can think about everything, about whether you are going to do, before you do that thing. Now, that's bad for them because you can't do that without wings...All you can do is do what you know has got to be done as right as you know how to do that thing. White people don't seem to know that. (88)

...he keeps changing the rules...Now, Chahlie will rule you to death. (16)

Authority seems to be central to whiteliness, as you might expect from a people who are raised to run things, or to aspire to that: belief in one's authority in matters practical, moral and intellectual exists in tension with the insecurity and hypocrisy that are essentially connected with the pretense of infallibility. This pretentiousness makes the whitely person simultaneously rude, condescending, overbearing and patronizing on the one hand, and on the other, weak, helpless, insecure and seeking validation of her or his goodness.

Drylongso: White people have got to bluff it out as rulers...[they] are always unsure of themselves. (99)

No matter what Chahlie do, he want his mama to pat him on the head and tell him how cute he is. (19)

...[I]n a very real sense white men never grow up. (100)

Hard on the outside, soft on the inside. (99)

Bridge: Socially...juvenile and tasteless. (99)

No responsibility to others. (70)

The dogmatic belief in whitely authority and rightness is also at odds with any commitment to truth.

Drylongso: They won't tell each other the truth, and the lies they tell each other sound better to them than the truth from our mouths. (29)

> As long as they can make someone say rough is
> smooth, they are happy...Like I told you,
> whitefolks don't care about what the truth
> is...It's like when you lie but so much, you
> don't know what the truth is. (21)

> You simply cannot be honest with white people.
> (45)

Bridge: White feminists have a serious problem with
truth and "accountability." (85)

And finally, whitely people make it clear to people of
other races that the last thing the latter are supposed to do is to
challenge whitely people's authority.

Bridge: [W]e are expected [by white women] to move,
charm or entertain, but not to educate in ways
that are threatening to our audiences. (71)

Margin: Though they expected us to provide first hand
accounts of black experience, they felt it was
their role to decide if these experiences were
authentic. (11)

Often in situations where white feminists aggressively attacked individual black women, they saw themselves as the ones
who were under attack, who were the victims. (13)

Drylongso: Most white people—anyways all the white
people I know—are people you wouldn't want
to explain anything to. (67)

No wonder whitely people have so much trouble learning, so much trouble receiving, understanding and acting on
moral or political criticism and demands for change. How can
you be a preacher who does not know right from wrong, a judge
who is an incompetent observer, a martyr who victimizes others,
a peace-maker who is the problem, an authority without authority, a grownup who is a child? How can someone who is
supposed to be running the world acknowledge their relative
powerlessness in some matters in any politically constructive
way? Any serious moral or political challenge to a whitely
person must be a direct threat to her or his very being.

Whiteliness and Class

What I have been exploring here, and calling "whiteliness," may sound to some like it is a character of middle class white people, or perhaps of middle class people whatever their race; it may sound like a class phenomenon, not a race phenomenon. Before addressing this question more deeply, I should just register that it is my impression, just looking around at the world, that white self-righteousness is not exclusive to the middle class. Many poor and working class white people are perfectly confident that they are more intelligent, know more, have better judgment and are more moral than Black people or Chicanos or Puerto Ricans, or Indians, or anyone else they view as not-white, and believe that they would be perfectly competent to run the country and to rule others justly and righteously if given the opportunity.

But this issue of the relation of whiteliness to class deserves further attention.

Though I think that what I am talking about *is* a phenomenon of race, I want to acknowledge a close inter-weaving and double-determination of manifestations and out-comes of race and of class, and to consider some of the things that give rise to the impression that what I'm calling whiteliness may really be just "middle-class-iness." One thing that has happened here is that the individual who contributed to the observations assembled in the preceding section as a "partici-pant observer" among white people (viz., the author of this analysis) is herself a lifelong member of the middle class. The whiteliness in which she has participated and about which she can write most vividly and authentically is that of her own kin, associates, and larger social group. This might, to a certain extent, bias that section's description of whiteliness toward a middle-class version of it.

Another reason that what I am calling whiteliness might appear to be a class character rather than a race one is that even if it is not peculiar to whites of the middle classes, it is nonetheless peculiarly suitable to them: it suits them to their jobs and social roles of managing, policing, training and disciplining, legislating and administering, in a capitalist bu-reaucratic social order.

Another interesting point in this connection is that the definition of a dominant race tends to fasten on and project an image of a dominant group within that race as *paradigmatic* of the race.[15] The ways in which individual members of that elite group enact and manifest their racedness and dominance would constitute a sort of norm of enacting and manifesting this racedness which non-elite members of the race would generally tend to assimilate themselves to. Those ways of enacting and manifesting racedness would also carry marks of the class position of the paradigmatic elite within the race, and these marks too would appear in the enactments of race by the non-elite. In short, the ways members of the race generally enact and stylistically manifest membership in the race would tend to bear marks of the class status of the elite paradigmatic members of the race.

I do not think whiteliness is just middle-class-ness misnamed. I think of whiteliness as a way of being which extends across ethnic, cultural, and class categories and occurs in ethnic, cultural, and class varieties—varieties which may tend to blend toward a norm set by the elite groups within the race. Whatever class and ethnic variety there is among white people, though, such niceties seem often to have no particular salience in the experience people of other races have with white people. It is very significant that the people of color from whose writings and narratives I have quoted in the preceding section often characterize the white people they talk about in part by class status, but they do not make anything of it. They do not generally indicate that class differences among white people make much difference to how people of color experience them.

Speaking of the oppression of women, Gayle Rubin noted its "endless variety and monotonous similarity."[16] There is great variety among the men of all the nationalities, races, religions and positions in various economies and polities, and women do take into account the particulars of the men they must deal with. But when our understanding of the world is conditioned by consciousness of sexism and misogyny, we see *also*, very clearly, the impressive and monotonous *lack* of variety among "masculinities." With my notion of whiteliness, I am reaching for the monotonous similarity, not the endless variety, in white folks' ways of being in the world. For various reasons, that monotonous similarity may have a middle-class cast to it, or my own perception of it may give it a middle-class cast, but I think that what I am calling "whiteliness" is a phenomenon of race. It is integral to what constructs and what is constructed by race, and only more indirectly related to class.

Feminism and Whiteliness

Being whitely, like being anything else in a sexist culture, is not the same thing in the lives of white women as it is in the lives of white men. The political significance of one's whiteliness interacts with the political significance of one's status as female or male in a male-supremacist culture. For the white men, a whitely way of being in the world is very harmonious with masculinity and their social and political situation. For white women it is, of course, all very much more complicated.

Femininity in white women is praised and encouraged but is nonetheless contemptible as weakness, dependence, feather-brainedness, vulnerability, and so on, but whiteliness in white women is unambivalently taken among white people as an appropriate enactment of a positive status. Because of this, for white women, whiteliness works more consistently than femininity does to disguise and conceal their negative value and low status as women, and at the same time to appear to compensate for it or to offset it.

Those of us who are born female and white are born into the status created by white men's hatred and contempt for women, but white girls aspire to Being and integrity, like anyone else. Racism translates this into an aspiration to whiteliness. The white girl learns that whiteliness is dignity and respectability; she learns that whiteliness is her aptitude for partnership with white men; she learns that partnership with white men is her salvation from the original position of Woman in patriarchy. Adopting and cultivating whiteliness as an individual character seems to put it in the woman's own power to lever herself up out of a kind of nonbeing (the status of woman in a male supremacist social order) over into a kind of Being (the status of white in white supremacist social order). But whiteliness does not save white women from the condition of *woman*. Quite the contrary. A white woman's whiteliness is deeply involved in her oppression as a woman and works against her liberation.

White women are deceived, deceive ourselves and will deceive others about ourselves, if we believe that by being whitely we can escape the fate of being the women of the white men. Being rational, righteous, and ruly (rule-abiding, and rule-enforcing) do for some of us some of the time buy a ticket to a higher level of material well-being than we might otherwise be permitted (though it is not dependable). But the reason, right, and rules are not of our own making; the white men may welcome our whiteliness as endorsement of their own values and as an expression of our loyalty to them (that is, as proof of their power over us), and because it makes us good helpmates to them. But if our whiteliness commands any respect, it is only in the sense that a woman who is chaste and obedient is called (by classic patriarchal reversal) "respectable."

It is commonly claimed that the Women's Movement in the United States, this past couple of decades, is a white women's movement. This claim is grossly disrespectful to the many feminists whom the label 'white' does not fit. But it is indeed the case that millions of white women have been drawn to and engaged in feminist action and theorizing, and this creative engagement did *not* arise from those women's being respected for their nice whitely ways by white men: it arose from the rape, battery, powerlessness, poverty or material dependence, spiritual depletion, degradation, harassment, servitude, insanity, drug addiction, botched abortions and murder of those very women, those women who are white.[17]

As doris davenport put it in her analysis of white feminists' racism:

> A few of us [third world women]...see beyond the so-called privilege of being white, and perceive white wimmin as very oppressed, and ironically, invisible... [I]t would seem that some white feminist could [see this] too. Instead, they cling to their myth of being privileged, powerful, and less oppressed...than black wimmin... Somewhere deep down (denied and almost killed) in the psyche of racist white feminists there is some perception of their real position: powerless, spineless, and invisible. Rather than examine it, they run from it. Rather than seek solidarity with wimmin of color, they pull rank within themselves.[18]

For many reasons it is difficult for women (of any intersection of demographic groups) to grasp the enormity, the full depth and breadth, of their oppression and of men's hatred and contempt for them. One reason is simply that the facts are so ugly and the image of that oppressed, despised and degraded woman so horrible that recognizing her as oneself seems to be accepting utter defeat. Some women, at some times, I am sure, must deny it to survive. But in the larger picture, denial (at least deep and sustained denial) of one's own oppression cuts one off from the appreciation of the oppression of others which is necessary for the connections one needs. This is what I think Cherríe Moraga is pointing out when she says:

> Without an emotional, heartfelt grappling with the source of our own oppression, without naming the enemy within ourselves and outside of us, no authentic, non-hierarchical connection among oppressed groups can take place.[19]

If white women are not able to ally with women of other races in the construction of another world, we will indeed remain, defeated, in this one.

White women's whiteliness does not deliver the deliverance we were taught it would; our whiteliness interferes with our ability to form necessary connections both by inhibiting and muddling our understanding of our own oppression as women, and by making us personally obnoxious and insufferable to many other women much of the time; it also is directly opposed to our liberation because it joins and binds us to our oppressors. By our whitely ways of being we enact partnership and racial solidarity with white men, we animate a social (if not also sexual) heterosexual union with white men, we embody and express our possession by white men.

A feminism that boldly names the oppression and degraded condition of white women and recognizes white men as its primary agents and primary beneficiaries—such a feminism can make it obvious to white women that the various forms of mating and racial bonding with white men do not and will never save us from that condition. Such a feminist understanding might free us from the awful confusion of thinking our whiteliness is dignity, and might make it possible for us to know that it is a dreadful mistake to think that our whiteliness earns us our personhood. Such knowledge can open up the possibility of practical understanding of whiteliness as a learned character (as we have already understood masculinity and femininity), a character by which we facilitate our own containment under the "protection" of white men, a character which interferes constantly and (often) conclusively with our ability to be friends with women of other races, a character by which we station ourselves as lieutenants and stenographers of white male power, a character which is not desirable in itself and neither manifests nor merits the full Being to which we aspire. A character by which, in fact, we both participate in and cover up our own defeat. We might then include among our strategies for change a practice of unlearning whiteliness, and as we proceed in this, we can only become less and less well-assimilated members of that racial group called "white." (I must state as clearly as possible that I do not claim that unbecoming whitely is the only thing white women need to do to combat racism. I have said that whiteliness is not the same thing as racism. I have no thought whatever that I am offering a panacea for the eradication of racism. I *do* think that *being* whitely interferes enormously with white women's attempts in general to be anti-racist.)

Disaffiliation, Deconstruction, Demolition

To deconstruct a concept is to analyze it in a way which reveals its construction—both in the temporal sense of its birth and development over time and in a certain cultural and political matrix, and in the sense of its own present structure, its meaning, and its relation to other concepts. One of the most impressive aspects of such an analysis is the revelation of the "contingency" of the concept, i.e. the fact that it is only the accidental collaboration of various historical events and circumstances that brought that concept into being, and the fact that there could be a world of sense without that concept in it. The other very impressive thing about such analyses is what they reveal of the complex and intense interplay of construction of concepts and construction of concrete realities. This interplay is what I take to be that phenomenon called the "social construction of reality."

In combination, the revelation of the historical contingency of a concept and the revelation of the intricacy of interplay between concept and the concrete lived reality give rise to a strong sense that "deconstruction" of a concept simultaneously dismantles the reality in whose social construction the evolution of the concept is so closely involved. But things do not work that way. In the first place, analyzing a concept and circulating the analysis among a few interested colleagues does not make the concept go away, does not dislodge it from the matrix of concepts in the active conceptual repertoire even of those few people, much less of people in general. In the second place, even if the deconstructive analysis so drains the concept of power for those few individuals that they can no longer use it, and perhaps their participation in the social constructions of which that concept is a part becomes awkward and halting (like tying your shoelaces while thinking directly about what you are doing), it still leaves those social constructions fully intact. Once constructed and assimilated, a social construct may be a pretty sturdy thing, not very vulnerable to erosion, decay, or demolition.[20] It is one thing to "deconstruct" a concept, another to dismantle a well-established, well-entrenched social construct. For example, Foucault's revelations about the arbitrariness and coerciveness of classifications of sexualities did not put an end to queer-bashing or to the fears lesbians and gay men have of being victims of a witch-hunt.

I am interested, as I suggested earlier in this essay, in the matter of how to translate the recognition of the social-constructedness of races into some practice of the freedom these contingencies seem to promise, some way to proceed by which people can be liberated from the concrete reality of races as they are determined by racism. But the social-constructedness of race and races in the racist state has very different meanings for groups differently placed with respect to these categories. The ontological freedom of categorical reconstruction may be generic, but what is politically possible differs for those differently positioned, and not all the politically possibilities for every group are desirable. Attempts by any group to act in this ontological freedom need to be informed by understanding of how the action is related to the possibilities and needs of the others.

I have some hope that if I can manage to refuse to enact, embody, animate this category—the white race—as I am supposed to, I can free up my energies and actions from a range of disabling confinements and burdens, and align my will with the forces which eventually will dissolve or dismantle that race as such. If it is objected that it is an exercise of white privilege to dissociate myself from the white race this way, I would say that in fact this project is strictly forbidden by the rules of white solidarity and white supremacy, and is *not* one of the privileges of white power. It may also be objected that my adoption or recommendation of this strategy implies that the right thing to do, in general, for everyone, is to dissolve, dismantle, bring an end to, races; and if this indeed is the implication, it can sound very threatening to some of the people whose races are thus to be erased. This point is well-made by Franz Fanon in a response to Jean-Paul Sartre, described by Henry Louis Gates, Jr.

> Reading Sartre's account of Négritude (as an antithesis preparatory to a "society without races," hence "a transition and not a conclusion"), Fanon reports "I felt I had been robbed of my last chance"..."Sartre, in this work, has destroyed black zeal..."[21]

The dynamic creative claiming of racial identities (and gender identity) that arose as devices of people's oppression has been a politically powerful and life-enhancing response of oppressed people in modern and contemporary times. For members of oppressor groups to suddenly turn around and decide to abolish races would be, it seems, genocide, not liberation. (I have a parallel unease about the project of dismantling the category of women, which some feminists seem to favor.)

But I am not suggesting that if white women should try to abandon the white race and contribute to its demolition, then women of other races should take the same approach to their racial categorization and their races. Quite the contrary. Approaches to the matter of dismantling a dominance-subordinance structure surely should be asymmetrical—they should differ according to whether one has been molded into its category of dominance or its category of subordination. My hope is that it may contribute to the demise of racism, if we upset the logical symmetry of race—if Black women, for instance, cultivate a racial identity and a distinctive (sexually egalitarian) Black community (and other women of racialized groups, likewise), while white women are undermining white racial identity and cultivating communities and agency among women along lines of affinity not defined by race. Such an approach would work toward a genuine redistribution of power.

Growing Room

The experience of feminists' unlearning femininity, and our readiness to require men to unlearn masculinity shows that it is thinkable to unlearn whiteliness. If I am right about all this, then, indeed, we even know a good deal about how to do it.

We know that white feminists have to inform ourselves exhaustively of its politics. We know we have to avoid, or be extremely alert in, environments in which whiteliness is particularly required or rewarded (e.g., academia). We know we have to *practice* new ways of being in environments which nurture different habits of feeling, perception, and thought, and that we will have to make these environments for ourselves since the world will not offer them to us. We know that the process will be collective and that this collectivity does not mean we will blend seamlessly with the others into a colorless mass; women unlearning femininity together have not become clones of each other or of those who have been valuable models. As feminists we have learned that we have to resist the temptation to encourage femininity in other women when, in moments of exhaustion and need we longed for another's sacrificial mothering or wifing. Similarly, white women have to resist the temptation to encourage whiteliness in each other when, in moments of cowardice or insecurity, we long for the comfort of "solidarity in superiority," or when we wish someone would relieve our painful uncertainty with a timely application of judgments and rules.

Seasoned feminists (white feminists along with feminists of other races) know how to transform consciousness. The first break-through is in the moment of knowing another way of being is possible. In this matter of a white woman's racedness, the possibility in question is the possibility of disengaging (on some levels, at least) one's own energies and wits from the continuing project of the social creation and maintenance of the white race, the possibility of being disloyal to that project by stopping constantly making oneself whitely. And this project should be a very attractive one to white women once we get it that it is the possibility of *not being whitely*, rather than the possibility of *being whitely*, that holds some promise of our rescuing ourselves from the degraded condition of women in white men's world.

[1] The working title during that period was "Ritual Libations and Points of Explosion," which referred to a remark made by Helene Wenzel in a review of my *Politics of Reality* which appeared in *The Women's Review of Books*, Vol.1, No.1, October, 1983. Wenzel said:

"Even when white women call third world women our friends, and they us, we still agonize over "the issue." The result is that when we write or teach about race, racism and feminism we tend either to condense everything we have to say to the point of explosion, or, fearing just that explosion, we sprinkle our material with ritual libations which evaporate without altering our own, or anyone else's consciousness."

And, coming down to cases, she continued: "Frye has fallen into both of these traps."

2 For some critical reflection on "wanting to do good," and on "not knowing how to act," see "A Response to *Lesbian Ethics*: Why Ethics?" in this volume.

3 Actually, what I think women of color have communicated in this matter is not so harsh as that. The point is that no one can do someone else's growing for her, that white women must not expect women of color to be *on call* to help, and that there is a great deal of knowledge to be gained by reading, interacting, paying attention, which white women need not ask women of color to supply. Some women of color have helped me a great deal (sometimes in spite of me).

4 Frye, *The Politics of Reality* (Freedom, CA: The Crossing Press, 1983), pp.115-116.

5 It is easy for a white person who is trying to understand white privilege and white power in white supremacist states to make the mistake of (self-servingly) exaggerating that power and privilege, assuming it is total. In this case, I was earlier making the mistake of thinking that white domination means that white people totally control the definition of race and the races. Reading bell hook's *Yearning* (Boston: South End Press, 1990), I awoke to the fact that afro-americans (and other racialized people) are engaged also in the definition of Black (and other "race" categories); white people have the power to enforce their own definitions in many (but not all) situations, but they are not the only people determining the meanings of race categories and race words, and what they determine for themselves (and enforce) is not necessarily congruent with what others are determining for *them*selves.

6 I want to thank María Lugones, whose palpably loving anger on this point made me take it seriously. See "Hablando Cara a Cara/Speaking Face to Face: An Exploration of Ethnocentric Racism" in Gloria Anzaldúa, editor, *Making Face, Making Soul: Haciendo Caras: Critical and Creative Perspectives by Women of Color* (San Francisco: aunt lute foundation press, 1990).

7 Singleton, Carrie Jane, "Race and Gender in Feminist Theory," SAGE, Vol VI, No. 1 (Summer 1989), p.15.

8 I am not unmindful here of the anxiety some readers may have about my reliance on a distinction between that which is physically given and that which is socially acquired. I could immensely complicate this passage by shifting from the material mode of talking about maleness and skin colors to the formal mode of talking about conceptions or constructions of maleness and skin colors. But it would not make anything clearer. It is perfectly meaningful to use the terms 'male' and 'white' (as a pigment word), while understanding that sex categories and color categories are "constructed" as the kinds of categories they are, i.e., physical categories, as opposed to social categories like *lawyer* or arithmetic categories like *ordinals*.

9 Moraga, Cherríe, and Gloria Anzaldúa, editors, *This Bridge Called My Back: Writing By Radical Women of Color* (Brooklyn, NY: Kitchen Table: Women of Color Press, 1981). I quote from writings by Barbara Cameron, Chrystos, doris davenport, and Mitsuye Yamada.

[10] hooks, bell, *Feminist Theory: From Margin to Center* (Boston: South End Press, 1985).

[11] Gewaltney, John Langston, *Drylongso: A Self-Portrait of Black America* (NY: Random House, 1983). I quote from statements by Jackson Jordan, Jr., Hannah Nelson, John Oliver, Howard Roundtree, Rosa Wakefield, and Mabel Lincoln.

[12] The people speaking in *Drylongso* were responding to questions put by an interviewer. The narratives as published do not include the questions, but the people clearly were asked in some manner to say something about how they see white people or what they think white people generally are like. Most of them but not every one, prefaced or appended their comments with remarks to the effect that they did not think white people were "like that" by birth or blood, but by being brought up a certain way in certain circumstances.

[13] "Identity: Skin Blood Heart," in *Yours in Struggle*, edited by Elly Bulkin, Minnie Bruce Pratt and Barbara Smith (Brooklyn: Long Haul Press, 1984).

[14] For more exploration of some of the meanings of this, see "Response to *Lesbian Ethics*: Why Ethics?" in this volume.

[15] Cf. Balibar, Etienne, "Paradoxes of Universality," translated by Michael Edwards in David Theo Goldberg, editor, *Anatomy of Racism* (Minneapolis: University of Minnesota Press, 1990), pp. 284-85, extracted from "Racisme et nationalism," in Etienne Balibar and Immanuel Wallerstein, *Race, Nation, Classe* (Paris: Editions La Decouverte, 1988).

[16] "The Traffic in Women," *Toward An Anthropology of Woman*, ed., Rayna R. Reiter (New York: Monthly Review Press, 1975), p.160.

[17] Carolyn Shafer is the one who brought to my attention the fact that there is a certain contradiction in claiming *both* that this stage of the women's movement was created by and belongs to white women *and* (on the grounds of the generally better material welfare of white women, compared to women of other races in the U.S.) that white women are not all that badly off and don't really know what suffering is about. If white women were as generally comfortable, secure and healthy as they might appear to some observers, they would not have participated as they have in an enormous movement whose first and most enduring issues are bodily integrity and economic self-sufficiency.

[18] "The Pathology of Racism: A Conversation with Third World Wimmin," *This Bridge Called My Back: Writings By Radical Women of Color*, ed., Cherríe Moraga and Gloria Anzaldúa (New York: Kitchen Table: Women of Color Press, 1981), pp.89-90.

[19] *This Bridge Called My Back: Writings by Radical Women of Color*, edited by Cherríe Moraga and Gloria Anzaldúa (NY: Kitchen Table: Women of Color Press, 1981), p.21.

[20] My lover Carolyn was explaining what I do for a living to our coheart Keyosha, and included an account of "deconstruction." Keyosha, a welder and pipefitter in the construction trades, said that wasn't a real word and offered "demolition" as the real word for this. Carolyn then had to admit (on my

behalf) that all this deconstructing did not add up to any demolition, and a made-up abstract word was probably suitable to this abstract activity.

[21] "Critical Remarks," *Anatomy of Racism*, ed., David Theo Goldberg (Minneapolis, MN: University of Minnesota Press, 1990), p.325.